Crafts for All Seasons

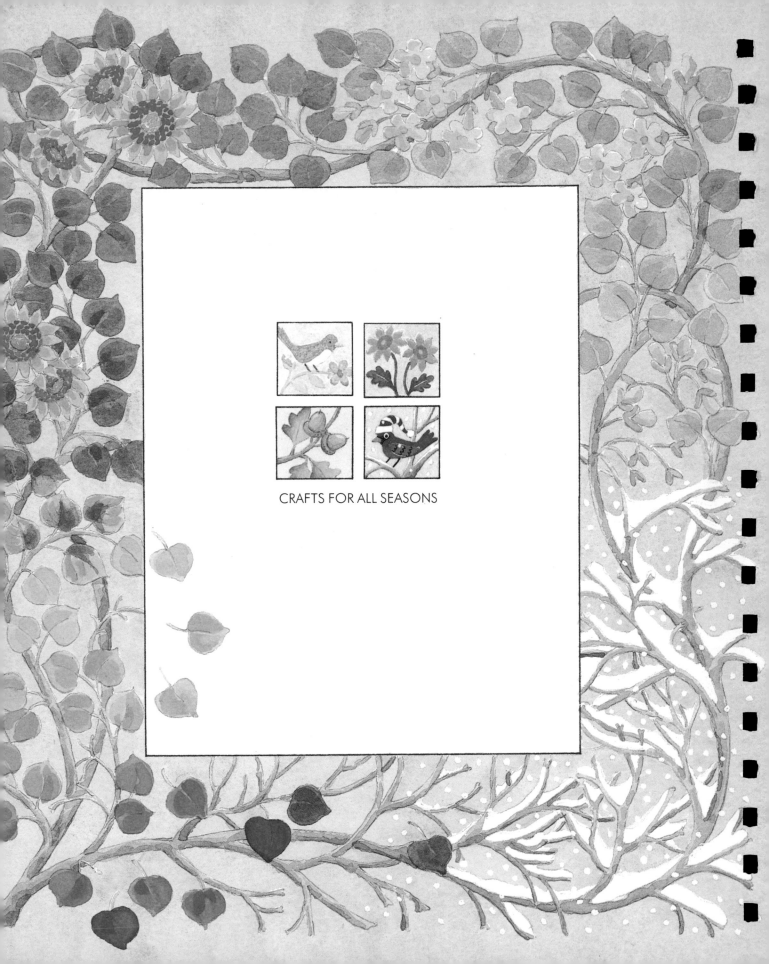

CRAFTS FOR ALL SEASONS

Crafts for all Seasons

KATHY ROSS

Illustrated by Vicky Enright

The Millbrook Press   Brookfield, Connecticut

For Tom—my man for all seasons.

Published by The Millbrook Press, Inc.
2 Old New Milford Road
Brookfield, Connecticut 06804
www.millbrookpress.com

Library of Congress Cataloging-in-Publication Data
Ross, Kathy (Katharine Reynolds), 1948–
Crafts for all seasons / Kathy Ross;
illustrated by Vicky Enright.
p. cm.
Summary: Presents instructions for easy-to-make craft projects with
seasonal themes.
ISBN 0-7613-1346-X
1. Handicraft—Juvenile literature. [1. Handicraft. 2. Seasons.] I.
Enright, Vicky, ill. II. Title
TT160 .R71412 2000   745.5—dc21   99–052760

1 3 5 4 2

Contents

Dear Crafters,

There are lots of times when it is fun to just stay indoors and work on a rewarding project. In this book, you will find just the right craft to keep you happily occupied, whether on a windy fall day, a frigid winter day, a rainy spring day, or a sticky hot summer day.

You can celebrate the cycle of the year with crafts that reflect the earth's seasonal changes and the holidays that are a treasured part of each of the four seasons. Whether you need a vase for your spring flowers, a cushion for a summer picnic, place cards for the Thanksgiving table, or a Christmas gift for your grandparents, just turn to the season of your choice and browse. The projects are as varied as the seasons they represent—practical items such as a photo album or picture frames, jewelry, greeting cards, holiday decorations, toys, and gifts. Once you decide on exactly the right project, then all you have to do is get out your scissors and paste and a few other easy-to-find craft supplies, and have fun!

Happy crafting!

Kathy Ross

Crafts
to make
in the
Fall

In many places leaves turn spectacular shades of yellow, red, and orange in the fall.

Fall Tree Lapel Pin

Here is what you need:

 four 12-inch (30-cm) brown pipe cleaners

 scissors

about twenty red, yellow, and orange flat buttons

safety pin

Here is what you do:

1 Hold three of the brown pipe cleaners together and bend them in half. Twist about 3 inches (8 cm) of the folded end of the pipe cleaners together to form a trunk for the tree. Spread the ends of the pipe cleaners out to form branches for the tree.

2 Cut the remaining pipe cleaner into 3-inch (8-cm) pieces. Wrap the pieces around the branches of the tree to make smaller branches.

(10

3 Slide the buttons onto the different branches of the tree to look like colorful leaves.

4 Slip the back of the safety pin between the twisted pipe cleaners to form a clasp so you can wear your tree as a lapel pin.

You might want to stand the tree in a ball of clay to use as a table decoration. Be sure to tape some felt to the bottom of the clay or put a dish under it so that the moist clay does not leave a mark on the table.

11)

This tree puppet changes color just like trees do each fall.

Changing Tree Puppet

Here is what you need:

  three 9-inch (23-cm) paper plates

orange and green poster paint and a paintbrush

orange and green tissue paper

brown construction paper

 scissors

 white glue

 stapler

 ruler

newspaper to work on

Here is what you do:

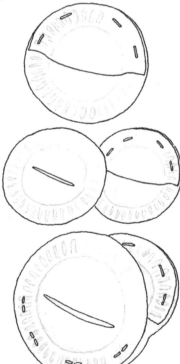

1 Cut one paper plate in half. Staple one half to the side of the second paper plate, keeping the staples around the outer edge of the plates.

2 Hold the last plate over the side of the plate with the half plate stapled to it. Cut a slit across the last plate about 1 inch (2½ cm) below the center of the plate so that your fingers will slip through the plate into the pocket formed by the half plate and the front plate. Staple the last plate in place making sure the cut is lined up with the opening to the half plate in between the two plates.

3 Turn the plates over so that the slit is across the back. Paint the front plate green. Cut lots of 1-inch (2½-cm) squares of green tissue paper. Crumple the squares and glue them over the front of the green to look like leaves. Let the paint and glue dry.

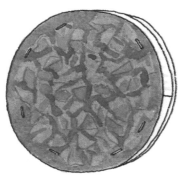

4 Fold the front, green plate down so that you can no longer see the green leaves. Paint the white plate surface orange. Cut lots of 1-inch (2½-cm) squares of orange tissue paper. Crumple the squares and glue them over the orange surface to look like leaves.

5 Cut a trunk for the tree puppet from brown construction paper. Glue the top of the trunk to the back of the tree, so it hangs down from the cut across the back of the puppet.

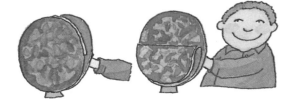

To use the puppet, slip your fingertips into the cut at the back of the tree. Flatten your hand to show the tree with green leaves. To change the leaves to orange, bend your fingers down to fold the green tree down and expose the orange tree.

13)

When you do this project, you end up with two fall decorations instead of one.

Leaf Print Banner and Window Leaves

Here is what you need:

- light colored fabric or paper
- stick or dowel
- yarn
- coffee filters
- markers (not permanent)
- scissors
- white glue
- paintbrush
- margarine tub for mixing
- plastic wrap
- water
- newspaper to work on

Here is what you do:

1 Cut a square of fabric or paper to use for your banner. Fold one end over the stick or dowel and glue it in place. Tie one end of a piece of yarn to each end of the stick to make a hanger for the banner.

(14

2 Cut two or three leaf shapes from coffee filters.

3 Color the leaves with markers. You can use patches of color or layers of color to color them. Avoid using too many dark colors, because they will run into the other colors and make them muddy.

4 Mix one part glue with one part water. Paint the colored side of each leaf with this mixture.

5 Place the wet leaves one at a time, face down, on the banner. Cover the leaf with plastic wrap and rub over it to transfer the leaf pattern onto the banner. You can get at least two prints from each leaf. Cover the banner with colorful leaf prints.

Save the colored leaves. When they are dry, they will look beautiful taped on a sunny window.

15)

This project is just what you need to both save and display your fall nature treasures.

Nature Collection Box

Here is what you need:

 shoe box

 five zip-to-close bags

poster paint and paintbrush

stapler

yellow construction paper

white glue

scissors

newspaper to work on

Here is what you do:

1 Paint the lid and the box and let them dry. You might want to make a label for the lid of the box that says your name and Nature Collection.

2 Cut a piece of construction paper to fit inside each of the plastic bags. Line each bag.

3 Cut a piece of construction paper to fit in the bottom of the box. Staple the paper to the side of one bag, stapling only the back of the bag behind the liner. Also, staple the paper along the bottom edge of the bag, through both sides of the bag.

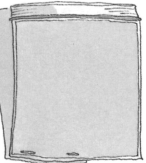

(16

4 Staple the side of the next bag to the side of the first bag, making sure that the bag openings face in the same direction. Staple all of the bags together to form a strip of five bags.

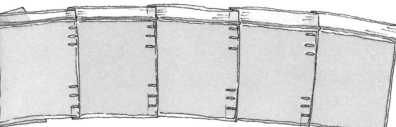

5 Cut a piece of construction paper to fit in the lid of the shoe box. Staple the piece to the side of the last bag in the row, stapling behind the liner. Also, staple the paper along the bottom edge of the bag, through both sides of the bag.

6 Glue the back paper on one end of the row of bags into the bottom of the shoe box. Glue the back paper on the other end of the row of bags into the lid of the shoe box. Let the glue dry.

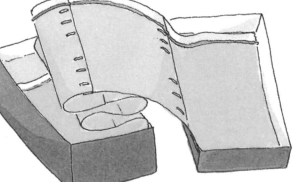

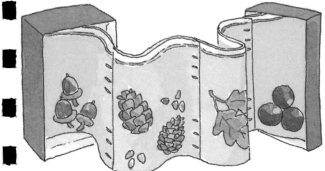

Use tape or glue to attach natural treasures such as leaves and seeds to the paper liners inside the plastic bags. To store your collection, just fold the bags, fan-style, into the shoe box. To display your collection, stand the box on one end and pull the lid out from the box to stand the bags up.

17)

Now that you are back in school, these magnets are just what you need to help display your best work.

Handprint Magnets

Here is what you need:

poster board

scissors

sticky-backed magnet

poster paint and a paintbrush

black permanent marker

Here is what you do:

1 Paint your right hand with poster paint and make a handprint on the poster board. Do the same thing with your left hand. Let the prints dry.

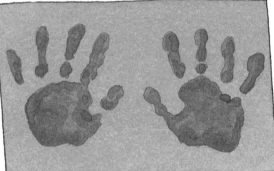

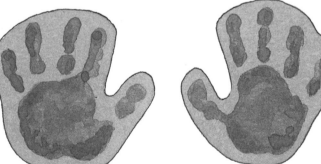

2 Cut around the outside of both handprints.

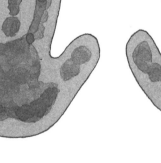

by Mike

3 Write the possessive form of your name on one hand and something like "work" or "masterpiece" on the other hand.

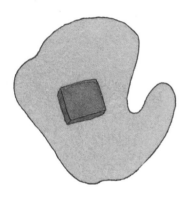

4 Put a piece of sticky-backed magnet on the back of each hand.

Put these handprints on your refrigerator to hold up your school and art work for all to appreciate.

19)

Make this clever picture frame to display your own school picture along with those of your friends.

School Bus Picture Frame

Here is what you need:

 empty watercolor paint box

yellow and white construction paper

 scissors

yellow yarn

white glue

masking tape

 markers

Here is what you do:

1 Trace around the paint box on the yellow paper. This will be the windows of the bus. Draw a bus shape without wheels around the windows. Cut out the bus shape. Cut out the window area of the bus shape.

2 Cut a 2-foot (60-cm) piece of yellow yarn. Open the paint box and thread the yarn inside the box around each side of the hinges. Tie the ends of the yarn together to make a hanger.

(20

3 Close the box. Put the bus shape down over the paint box so that the box becomes windows for the bus. Turn the bus over and use masking tape to hold the bus in place around the paint box.

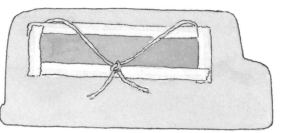

4 Cut wheels for the bus from the white paper. Glue them in place at the bottom of the bus.

5 Cut a piece of white paper to fit inside the paint box windows. Put a strip of masking tape across the bottom of the box to create a better gluing surface. Glue the white paper liner inside the box.

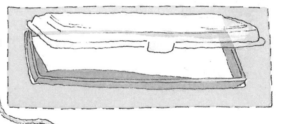

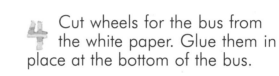

6 Use markers to decorate the bus any way you wish.

Use small pieces of rolled masking tape to tape school pictures in the paint box windows of the bus to look like passengers looking out.

21)

If you made one or more crow puppets, you may want to make this scarecrow to keep them from becoming too big a nuisance.

Scarecrow Rod Puppet

Here is what you need:

two or more old neckties

yellow cupcake wrapper

old white sock

two buttons

yellow yarn

10-inch (25-cm)- and 14-inch (35-cm)-long sticks

felt and fabric scraps

white glue or blue glue gel

scissors

Here is what you do:

1 Cut a 4-inch (10-cm) piece from the toe of the sock. Cut the rest of the sock into pieces and use them to stuff the cut toe end. This will be the head of the scarecrow. Use a piece of yarn to tie the stuffed head closed around one end of the longer stick.

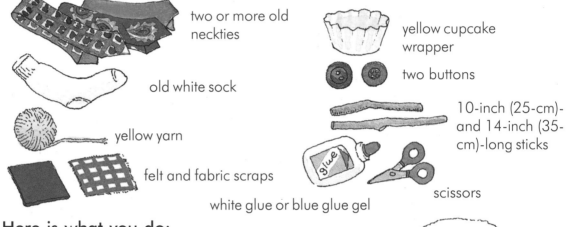

2 Cut a 12-inch (30-cm) rectangle from the wide end of a tie. Fold the piece in half and cut a small slit in the center of the fold for a neck hole. Put the bottom end of the stick down into the neck hole, then slide the tie up under the head of the scarecrow to make the body.

(22

3 Cut a 10-inch (25-cm) strip from the thin end of a tie for arms. If you keep the point, cut the other end into a point too. Slide the short stick through the tie arms to support them. Glue the arms between the top front and back of the body so that they stick out on each side of the scarecrow.

4 Cut a 12-inch (30-cm) piece from the thin end of another tie. Trim off the point. Fold the piece in the center to make a V shape. Glue the point of the V between the front and back of the bottom of the body so that the two ends of the tie piece hang down to form legs for the scarecrow.

5 Cut bits of yellow yarn for straw. Glue the yarn pieces sticking out from the bottom of the head and the ends of the arms and legs.

6 Glue the two buttons on the head of the scarecrow for eyes. Cut a triangle nose from felt and glue it on. Glue the yellow cupcake wrapper on the scarecrow's head for a straw hat.

7 Cut patches from the fabric and felt scraps. Glue them on the scarecrow.

Can your scarecrow keep those pesky crows out of the corn?

23)

Rosh Hashanah, the Jewish New Year, is celebrated in the fall.

Apple New Year Card

Here is what you need:

- two 6-inch (15-cm) paper plates
- apple seeds
- red poster paint and a paintbrush
- masking tape
- newspaper to work on
- black marker
- yellow, brown, and green construction paper
- scissors
- white glue
- hole punch
- plastic grocery bag
- yarn

Here is what you do:

1 Paint the back of both paper plates red and let them dry.

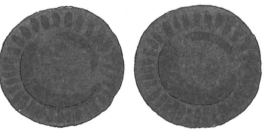

2 Stack the two plates together with the red bottoms facing out on each side, to form the front and back of an apple. Punch a hole through the edge of both plates. Tie the two plates together loosely through the holes with a piece of yarn.

(24

3 Cut a stem and leaf for the apple from the construction paper. Glue the stem and leaf to the top edge of one side of the apple so that they conceal the hole and yarn tie.

4 Cut a bee from yellow paper. Use the black marker to add details to the bee. Cut wings for the bee from the plastic grocery bag. Wrap the center of the wings with a thin piece of masking tape. Glue the taped portion of the wings to the back of the bee.

5 Open the apple card up and write a New Year's greeting inside and sign your name. Glue apple seeds down the center of the message so that the white side of the paper plate looks like the inside of an apple.

Wishing you
a sweet
New Year
Love
Ira

Make apple New Year cards for all your friends and family.

25)

When the giant sunflowers of summer start dropping seeds, you know that fall is here.

Sunflower Seeds Bowl

Here is what you need:

 sunflower seeds

 small plastic margarine tub

white glue

craft stick

Here is what you do:

1 Fill the tub half full of sunflower seeds.

2 Add enough white glue to completely coat all of the seeds. Use the craft stick to mix the seeds and the glue completely.

3 Shape the gluey seeds into a bowl shape by pressing seeds around the sides of the tub and flat on the bottom. Let the glue dry completely. This could take several days.

4 When the glue is dry carefully peel the seed bowl out of the margarine tub. If the bottom is still a little gluey, just turn the bowl over and let it dry.

This little bowl would make a lovely gift for someone you know.

Stuffed Apple 🍎

Here is what you need:

old white sock

rubber band

fiberfill

green yarn

red and green poster paint and a paintbrush

scissors

hole punch

green felt scrap

Styrofoam tray for drying

Here is what you do:

1 Cut a 5-inch (13-cm) piece from the toe end of the sock.

2 Stuff the toe with fiberfill to make a round apple shape. Close the opening of the sock with a rubber band.

3 Paint the round part of the apple red. Paint the excess sock above the rubber band green and twist it into a stem while it is still wet.

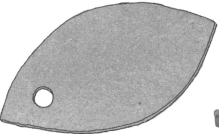

4 Cut a leaf shape from the green felt. Punch a hole at the base of the leaf.

5 Cut an 8-inch (20-cm) piece of green yarn. Thread the leaf onto the yarn and tie it to the base of the stem of the apple. Wrap the yarn around the rubber band to conceal it. Tie the ends together to hold the leaf and yarn in place.

Make just one apple or several to display in a basket or bowl.

29)

Cork Squirrel

Here is what you need:

 cork

 two small wiggle eyes

cotton ball

tiny brown pom-pom

 brown paper scrap

 brown marker

 scissors

white glue

Here is what you do:

1 Stretch the cotton ball out to make a tail for the squirrel. Dab the cotton with the side of the brown marker to add color. Glue the tail up one side of the cork.

(30

2 Glue the two wiggle eyes and the pom-pom nose to the top front of the cork.

3 Cut two pointy ears from the brown paper. Glue the ears to the front of the squirrel above the eyes.

Make a large family of squirrels using corks of varying shapes and sizes.

Columbus Day Hat

Here is what you need:

white and blue construction paper and other colors

scissors

stapler

white glue

markers

1 Cut a 2½-inch (6-cm)-wide band from the blue construction paper. Make it long enough to fit around your head. You may need to staple two bands of paper together to make a strip that is long enough. Cut the top of the band into waves so that it looks like the ocean. Staple the two ends of the band together.

(32

2 Cut three ships from different color papers. Label them *Niña, Pinta,* and *Santa Maria,* the names of Columbus's three ships. Cut sails for each ship from the white paper and glue them in place.

3 Glue the bottom of each ship around the inside band to look like they are sailing on the ocean.

You might want to write something on your band like "Happy Columbus Day" or the verse that helps you remember the year: "In fourteen hundred and ninety two, Columbus sailed the ocean blue…"

33)

Firefighter Down the Pole

Here is what you need:

cardboard paper towel tube

white paper

aluminum foil

cellophane tape

red yarn

markers

stapler

scissors

Here is what you do:

1 Cover the tube with aluminum foil to make the pole. Tuck the extra foil into each end of the tube. Use tape to hold the foil in place around the tube.

2 Cut a piece of yarn about 2½ times as long as the tube. String one end of the yarn through the tube and knot the ends together at the bottom. Leave 4 or 5 inches (10 or 13 cm) of extra yarn at each end of the tube after the knot. Make sure the yarn is loose enough so that it slides easily through the tube.

(34

3 Use the markers to draw a 4-inch (10-cm)-tall firefighter on the white paper. Cut around the firefighter picture.

4 Staple the firefighter above the yarn knot outside the tube.

To slide the firefighter down the pole, just pull on the excess yarn below the knot.

35)

Books Bookmark

Here is what you need:

 book catalog or flyer

 cereal box cardboard or posterboard

yarn

 white glue

hole punch

clear packing tape

scissors

Here is what you do:

1 Cut five book cover pictures from a book club flyer or catalog.

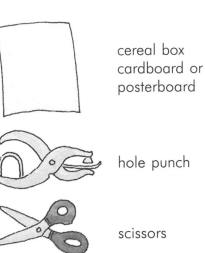

2 Glue the five pictures to the cardboard in a strip formation to make a bookmark. Let the glue dry, then cover the front of the bookmark area with clear packing tape to protect it.

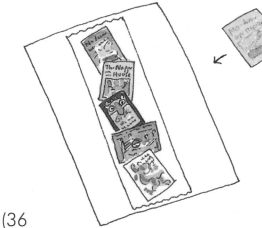

3 Cut the bookmark out. Punch a hole in the top of the bookmark.

4 Cut an 8-inch (20-cm) piece of yarn. Thread the yarn through the hole and tie the two ends together leaving two 1-inch (2½-cm)-long ends. Cut two 2-inch (5-cm)-long pieces of yarn. Tie the two together in the center using the ends of the yarn on the bookmark. Unravel the yarn ends to make a tassel at the end of the bookmark.

Watch your school book club flyers for favorite titles to use in making your own personal bookmark.

37)

This pumpkin is so nice and squishy,
you can use it for a pillow.

Soft Sculpture Pumpkin

Here is what you need:

 two pairs of old
pantyhose

 orange and green
poster paint and
a paintbrush

Styrofoam tray for drying

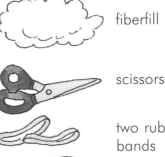 fiberfill

scissors

two rubber
bands

stapler

Here is what you do:

1 Cut the four legs off the pantyhose.
Arrange the legs crossing over each
other at the center like the spokes of a
wheel. Staple the legs together at the
point where they all cross over each other.

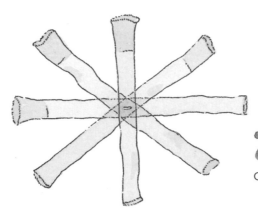

2 Cut the toe end off the foot of the
pantyhose so that all the legs are
open at the ends.

3 Stuff all eight sections of pantyhose with fiberfill. Leave about 6 inches (15 cm) at the end of each stocking unstuffed.

4 Pull the eight sections up and around to the center to form a pumpkin. Hold the sections together with a rubber band.

5 Braid the excess stocking ends together to make a stem for the pumpkin. Hold the braided stem in place with another rubber band.

6 Paint the pumpkin orange and the stem green. Let the project dry on the Styrofoam tray.

You can turn this pumpkin into a jack-o'-lantern by gluing on a face cut from black felt.

39)

Teddy Bear Cave

Here is what you need:

 large brown grocery bag

 fiberfill

stapler

white glue

scissors

white paper

marker

Here is what you do:

1 Cut about 4 inches (10 cm) off the top of the grocery bag.

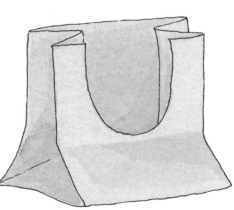

2 Cut an arched cave opening from one side of the bag.

3 Fold the two sides of the bag together and fold 1 inch (2½ cm) of the edge over. Staple along the edge to hold the fold in place.

4 Pop the bag open to form a cave for your teddy bear to winter in. Glue some fiberfill snow along the top of the cave and along the bottom opening.

5 Make a sign for the cave that says Good night, Mr. Bear! See you in the spring! You might want to line the bottom of the cave with some dry leaves to make it comfy.

Goodnight Mr. Bear! See you in the spring.

Don't worry about not seeing your teddy bear for several months. Bears often wake up during the winter months and come out and wander around a little before going back to sleep.

41)

FLORIDA BOUND!

travel book

sunflower seeds

sun tan lotion

Make this flag magnet in honor of Veteran's Day.

Flag Magnet

Here is what you need:

26 toothpicks

red marker

white glue

plastic lid for drying

scrap of blue construction paper

scissors

tiny gold star sequins or glitter

strip of sticky-backed magnet

Here is what you do:

1 Use the marker to color 14 toothpicks red.

2 Arrange them on the plastic lid starting with two red toothpicks across the top, then two natural colored toothpicks, alternating two of each color to make stripes of the flag. Our flag has 7 red stripes and 6 white ones.

3 Cover the toothpicks with a layer of white glue to hold them together. Do not flood the project with glue or the red marker will run.

(42

4 Cut a 1-inch (2½-cm) square of blue paper to glue on the upper left corner of the flag.

5 Cover the blue paper with glue and sprinkle it with the tiny stars. If you do not have stars you can dot the paper with glue then sprinkle it with glitter. You probably won't be able to fit all 50 stars on this tiny flag.

6 When the flag has dried completely peel the flag off the lid. Use scissors to trim off any excess glue.

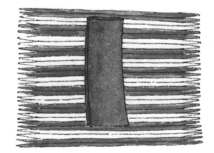

7 Stick a piece of sticky-back magnet on the back of the flag.

Put this flag on your refrigerator as a reminder of all the men and women who have served our country.

Tennis Ball Turkey

Here is what you need:

 old tennis ball

craft feathers

one bump of orange chenille-type pipe cleaner

two small wiggle eyes

buttons or corn kernels

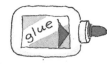 brown poster paint and a paintbrush

paint stirrer stick

white glue

Styrofoam egg carton for drying

Here is what you do:

1 Ask an adult to cut a 1-inch (2½-cm) slit in the tennis ball.

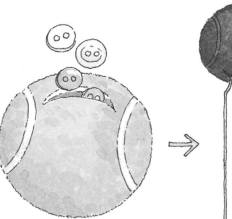

2 Squeeze the slit on each side to open the ball enough to drop in some buttons or corn kernels to make the ball a shaker. Slide the end of the paint stirrer into the cut so that the shaker has a handle.

(44

3 Bend the end of the orange bump chenille down to form a turkey head. Glue the head to the front of the ball. Glue the two wiggle eyes on each side of the head.

4 Glue colorful craft feathers across the back of the turkey for tail feathers.

5 Glue a craft feather on each side the turkey for wings.

When the glue has dried, your turkey will be ready to shake in time to your favorite Thanksgiving songs.

45)

These pilgrims work well as party hats or table decorations.

 PARTY HAT PILGRIMS

Here is what you need:

 two old cone-shaped party hats

 black poster paint and a paintbrush

 white, black, blue, yellow, and skin-colored construction paper

yarn in a hair color

white ribbon

markers

scissors

white glue

newspaper to work on

Here is what you do:

1 Paint the two party hats black and let them dry.

2 Cut two 3- by 4-inch (8- by 10-cm) rectangles of white paper for collars. Fold each collar in half and cut a neck hole. Slide each collar over the point of one hat and down about 1 inch (2½ cm). Cut a narrow triangle from the front of each collar.

(46

3 Cut two 2-inch (5-cm) circles from the skin-colored paper for the heads. Draw a boy's face on one and a girl's face on the other with markers. Glue a head to the point of each hat above the collar.

4 Cut rectangle arms from the black paper for each pilgrim. Cut a white paper cuff to glue to the end of each arm. Cut hands from the skin-colored paper to glue at the end of each cuff. Glue the top of each arm to one side of each pilgrim.

5 To finish the girl pilgrim: Cut a rectangle of white paper for an apron and glue it to the front of the girl pilgrim. Cut three 1- by 2-inch (2½- by 5-cm) rectangles. Glue one on each side of the head, tipped out slightly, and one at the top of the head to form a bonnet. Tie a bow with the white ribbon and glue it at the chin. Glue on snips of yarn for hair.

6 To finish the boy pilgrim: Cut a belt from the blue paper and a belt buckle from the yellow paper. Glue them in place across the front of the boy pilgrim. Cut a hat from the black construction paper and glue it on the head. Decorate the hat with a belt and buckle cut from the blue and yellow paper. Cut some snips of yarn to glue on for hair.

What a charming pair of pilgrims!

47)

The cornucopia is a symbol of the plentiful food that we give thanks for at Thanksgiving time.

Cornucopia Place Cards

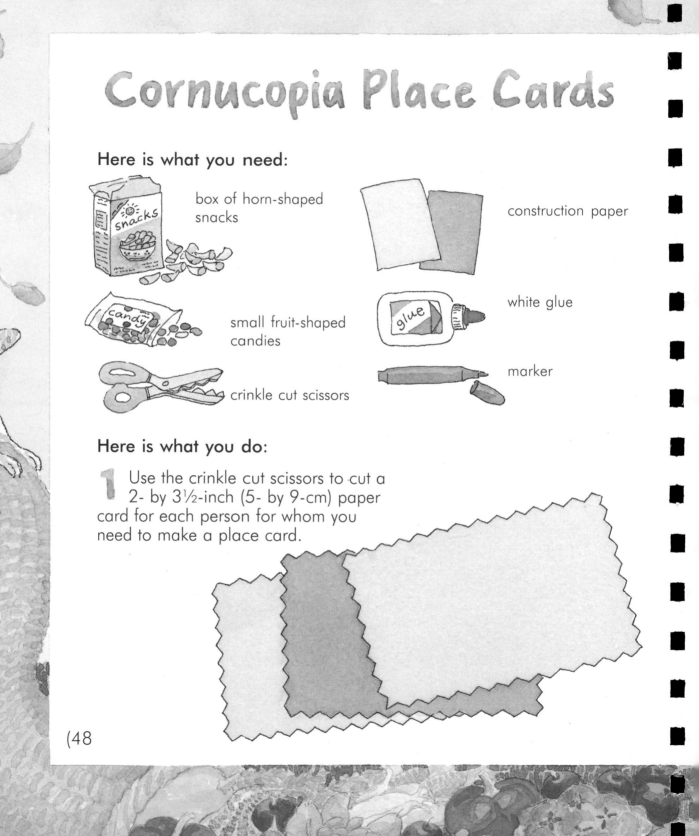

Here is what you need:

box of horn-shaped snacks

small fruit-shaped candies

crinkle cut scissors

construction paper

white glue

marker

Here is what you do:

1. Use the crinkle cut scissors to cut a 2- by 3½-inch (5- by 9-cm) paper card for each person for whom you need to make a place card.

(48

2 Glue a horn-shaped snack in the top left-hand corner of each card for a cornucopia.

3 Glue three or four little candies spilling out of the horn.

Kathy

Daniel

Sarah

Use the marker to write the name of each guest on a place card.

49)

(50

Crafts
to make
in the
Winter

Snowman Pin

Here is what you need:

- margarine tub for mixing
- white glue
- white poster paint and a paintbrush
- peanut
- Styrofoam tray for drying
- scissors
- tablespoon
- salt
- black and orange construction paper scraps
- ruler
- red yarn
- safety pin

Here is what you do:

1 In the margarine tub, mix a few drops of glue into a tablespoon of white paint. Paint the peanut white for the body of the snowman. Sprinkle the wet paint with salt and lean the peanut against the edge of the Styrofoam tray to dry.

(52

2 Cut a hat, eyes, and buttons for the snowman from the black paper. Cut a carrot nose from the orange paper. Glue the pieces onto the peanut snowman.

3 Cut a 5-inch (13-cm) piece of red yarn. Tie the yarn around the peanut snowman to make a scarf. Secure the scarf with glue. Trim the ends to a length that looks right for your snowman.

4 Slip the back of a safety pin through the yarn scarf at the back of the snowman.

Wear this little snowman on your coat or shirt. This snowman is happy indoors or out.

53)

Even if it doesn't snow where you live, you can make a snowman.

Jar Snowman

Here is what you need:

 large plastic jar with lid

scissors

orange felt scrap

fiberfill

large red pom-pom

four buttons

 white glue

two twigs

masking tape

Here is what you do:

1 Soak the jar in warm water to remove the label and any excess glue.

2 Stuff the jar with fiberfill to make the body of the snowman.

(54

3 Slip two buttons between the side of the jar and the fiberfill for the snowman's buttons. Cut a nose from the orange felt and slip it in the jar above the buttons. Put two more buttons above the nose for the eyes. Slip a twig into each side of the jar for the arms of the snowman.

4 Put the lid on the jar. Put a small piece of masking tape on the top center of the lid to create a better gluing surface. Glue the pom-pom in the center of the lid to make it look like a winter hat.

You might want to use cut paper or small stones for your snowman's eyes and buttons.

55)

Tiny Tree Ornament

Here is what you need:

 green yarn

scissors

ruler

craft stick

white glue

Styrofoam tray for drying

red felt scrap

colorful round- and star-shaped sequins

green rickrack

Here is what you do:

1 Wrap green yarn around your hand about thirty times. Slide the yarn off your hand and cut the end off from the main ball of yarn. Cut through the yarn loops twice so that you have two equal bunches of yarn.

2 Cut a 6-inch (15-cm)-long piece of yarn. Glue the two ends of the yarn about half way down one side of the craft stick so that a loop forms a hanger at one end of the stick.

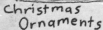
Christmas Ornaments

3 Rub glue all over one side of the craft stick. Lay the stick down on the tray and glue one of the piles of yarn strands across all of the stick except for one inch at the bottom. Turn the stick over and cover the other side in the same way, using the second pile of yarn. Let the glue dry.

4 Trim the yarn on each side to form a triangle-shaped tree. Rub glue over both sides of the tree and glue the trimmed-off bits of yarn back onto the tree to make it look shaggy.

5 Cut a base for each side of the tree from the red felt. Glue the two felt pieces together with the stick in the middle.

6 Choose one side of the tree to be the front of the ornament. Decorate the tree with the round- and star- shaped sequins. Decorate the red felt base with rickrack.

You might have some other ideas for how you want to trim your tree ornament.

Turn old lipstick tops into charming little trims for the Christmas tree.

Christmas Candy Ornament

Here is what you need:

gold lipstick top

green yarn or thin ribbon

scissors

clear plastic wrap

ruler

red or gold string or embroidery floss

Here is what you do:

1 Wrap the gold lipstick top in a piece of clear plastic wrap.

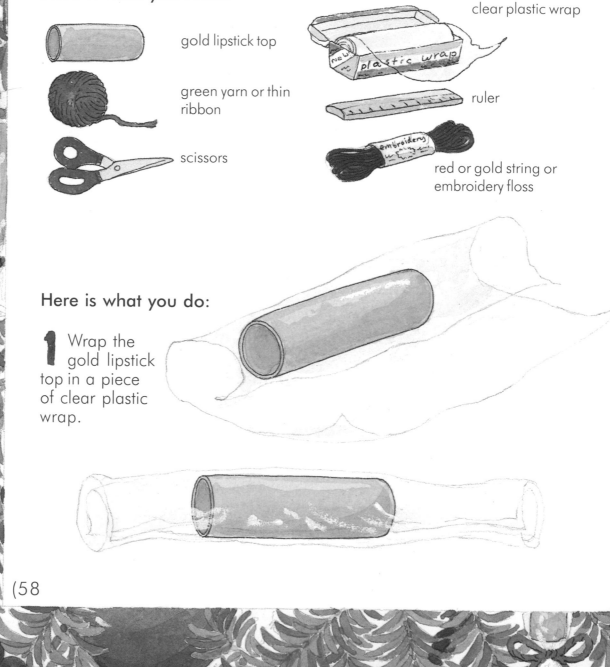

2 Tie each open end of the wrap closed with a piece of pretty ribbon or yarn tied in a bow.

3 Trim the ends of the plastic wrap so that they are even.

4 Cut a 5-inch (13-cm) length of string or floss. Slip one end of the string under the yarn at one end of the ornament. Tie the two ends of the string together to make a hanger for the ornament.

Hang this pretend candy up high so no one will try to eat it!

59)

Make this banner to decorate your house for the Hanukkah season.

Dreidel Banner

Here is what you need:

 scissors

ruler

blue and silver trims

 9- by 12-inch (23- by 30-cm) piece of blue felt

 cereal box cardboard

two silver sparkle stems

 white glue

two old neckties

large gold or silver sequins

Here is what you do:

1 Cut a 1½-inch (3-cm)-wide strip of cardboard 9 inches (23 cm) long to form a support for the top of the banner. Cut a piece of trim about 2 feet (60 cm) long and tie the ends together to form a hanger for the banner. Fold one 9-inch side of the felt over the hanger and the cardboard support and glue them in place.

2 Measuring from the point of each necktie, cut a piece from the wide end 4¼-inches (11 cm) long. The two cut pieces will be the dreidels for the banner.

3 Cut a sparkle stem in half. Fold each piece in half to form a handle for each dreidel. Glue a handle between the front and back of the tie at the top of each dreidel shape. Glue the two dreidels on the blue banner.

4 Shape one of the Hebrew letters found on a real dreidel out of pieces of sparkle stem. Glue a letter to the front of each dreidel.

5 Decorate the dreidels and the top and bottom of the banner by gluing on pretty trims.

6 Glue three or four sequins to each corner of the banner to look like gelt (money).

Spin, dreidel, spin!

61)

Make a corn magnet for Kwanzaa.

Ear of Corn Magnet

Here is what you need:

scissors

ruler

small-size bubble wrap

margarine tub and craft stick for mixing

sticky-back magnet

water

cereal box cardboard

yellow and brown tissue paper

white glue

Styrofoam tray for drying

3 INCHES

Here is what you do:

1 Cut a 3-inch (8-cm) -tall corn shape from the cardboard.

2 Cut a piece of bubble wrap to fit over one side of the corn shape to make the corn kernels.

3 Mix three parts of glue to one part of water in the margarine tub and mix with the craft stick.

4 Cut some strips of brown tissue paper about 2½ inches (6 cm) long and about 1 inch (2½ cm) wide. Glue the strips sticking out from the top of the corn to form the husks.

5 Cover the front of the corn with glue and glue the bubble wrap to the corn shape, covering the bottom edges of the brown husks.

6 Cut a piece of yellow tissue paper large enough to wrap around the corn shape to cover the front and the back of the corn. Dip the yellow tissue paper in the watery glue, then wrap it around the corn to cover it.
Let the project dry completely on the Styrofoam tray.

7 Put a piece of sticky-back magnet on the back of the corn.

You might want to make your mom an ear of corn magnet for each child in your family.

63)

Confetti Noise Maker

Here is what you need:

 small plastic
detergent bottle

scissors

thin ribbon

 confetti

three or more
jingle bells

 ruler

Here is what you do:

1 Cut an 18-inch (46-cm) piece
of ribbon. String three or more
jingle bells onto the ribbon. Tie the
ribbon and bells around the bottle.
Tie the two ends of the ribbon
together to make a wrist hanger
for the bottle.

64

2 Fill the bottle with confetti.

Bring in the new year by shaking your bottle to ring the bells and toss the confetti.

65)

Cold winter weather means ice skating.

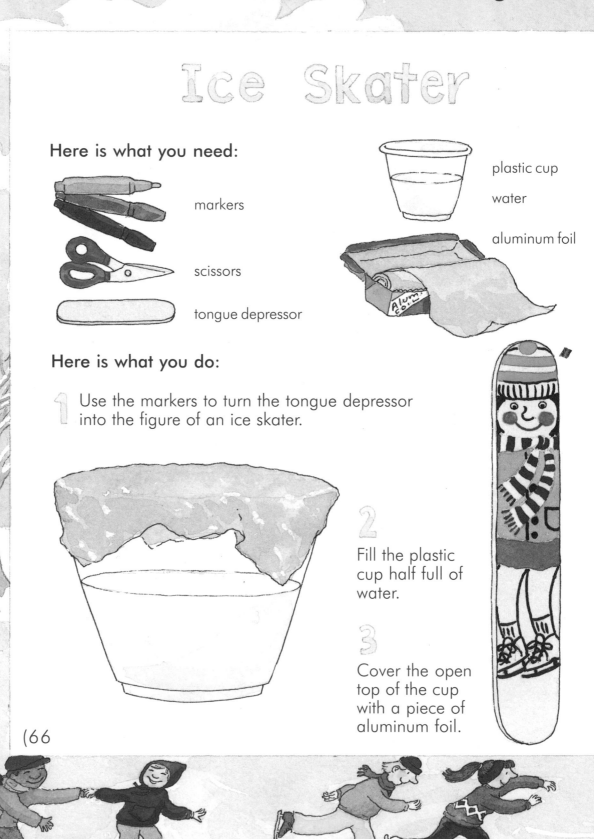

Ice Skater

Here is what you need:

markers

scissors

tongue depressor

plastic cup

water

aluminum foil

Here is what you do:

1 Use the markers to turn the tongue depressor into the figure of an ice skater.

2 Fill the plastic cup half full of water.

3 Cover the open top of the cup with a piece of aluminum foil.

4. Carefully cut a slit in the center of the foil. Slide the feet of the ice skater figure down through the slit so that it is standing straight up in the center of the cup.

5. Place the cup in the freezer or outdoors until the water has completely frozen.

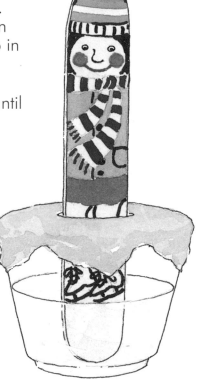

6. Run the outside of the cup under warm water until the ice skater pops out of the cup.

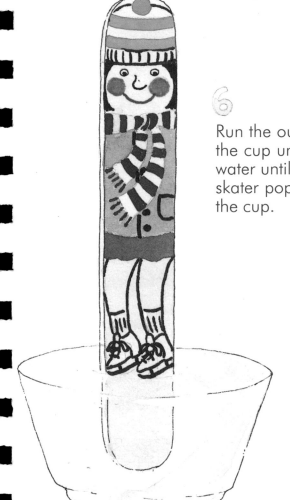

This ice skater will skate across a bare floor at a surprising speed. You might want to make more than one skater and race them. The ice base will, of course, melt after a while and you will need to freeze a new base for the skater.

Remember that this skater should only be used on a waterproof floor, not on wooden floors because the water might stain the wood.

This little snowman belongs indoors, not outdoors.

Baggy Snowman

Here is what you need:

large-size plastic food bag

Styrofoam packing pieces

string

scissors

orange and black construction paper scraps

two twigs

ruler

sock

white glue

pom-pom

fabric scrap

Here is what you do:

1 Fill the bottom half of the bag with Styrofoam pieces. Tie the bag closed with string to form the base of the snowman.

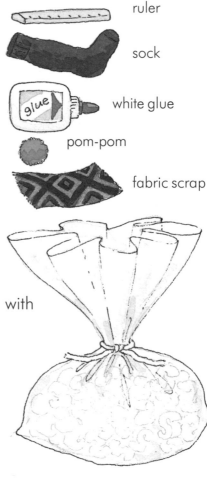

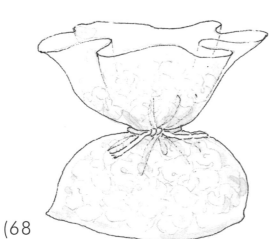

2 Fill the upper part of the bag with enough Styrofoam pieces to make a head for the snowman that is smaller than the body.

(68

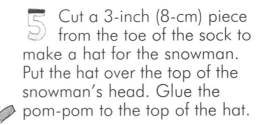

3 Cut two eyes for the snowman from black paper. Cut a carrot nose from the orange paper. Arrange the face pieces inside the bag on one side to form a face for the snowman. Tie the top of the bag shut.

4 Poke a twig into each side of the snowman's body to make arms.

5 Cut a 3-inch (8-cm) piece from the toe of the sock to make a hat for the snowman. Put the hat over the top of the snowman's head. Glue the pom-pom to the top of the hat.

6 Cut a scarf for the snowman from the fabric scrap. Tie the scarf around the snowman's neck.

This snowman may be so light that it will tumble away at the slightest breeze, but at least it will never melt!

69)

By January it is hard for the winter
birds to find food on their own.

Bird in the Snow
Table Decoration

Here is what you need:

clear plastic cup

forked twig small enough to
fit inside the cup

two tiny
wiggle eyes

Styrofoam packing
worm

scissors

cereal box
cardboard

white glue

birdseed

blue poster paint
and a paintbrush

blue and yellow
construction paper
scraps

fiberfill

Styrofoam tray
for drying

masking tape

blue trim

pencil

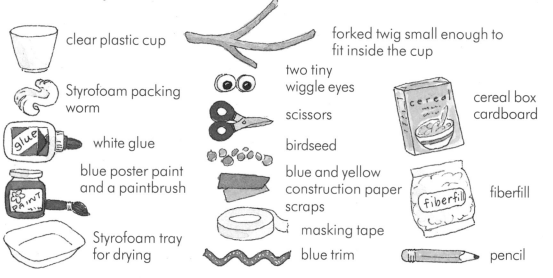

Here is what you do:

1 Carefully slide one branch of the
twig through one end of the Styrofoam
piece. Tip the piece up to look like a bird
perched on a branch. Do this before you
paint the bird because you might split
the Styrofoam and need to use another
one. Secure the perched bird with glue.

2 Paint the bird blue. Let the project
dry on the Styrofoam tray.

(70

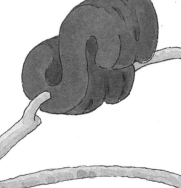

RECYCLING
Town of Bridge

3 Cut wings for the bird from the blue paper and a beak from the yellow paper. Glue the wings to the back of the bird. Glue the beak on the head of the bird. Glue two wiggle eyes above the beak.

4 Trace around the open end of the cup on the cardboard. Cut out the traced circle.

5 Glue the fiberfill to the circle for snow. Glue the branch with the bird on top of the snow. Glue some birdseed in the snow.

6 Cover the rim of the cup with masking tape to create a better gluing surface. Put glue around the opening of the cup and glue it over the bird in the snow.

7 Cover the masking tape around the bottom of the cup with glue, then decorate it with trim.

What a pretty reminder to feed the birds!

Martin Luther King Jr. wanted people of all races to get along together.

Friends Pin

Here is what you need:

old puzzle pieces

Styrofoam tray for drying

brown and pink poster paint (or two different colors for skin tones) and a paintbrush

masking tape

pin backing

white glue

Here is what you do:

1 Find two puzzle pieces that look like little people with a round head on top, arms on each side, and legs at the bottom.

2 Paint each piece a different skin color. Let the pieces dry on the Styrofoam tray.

(72

3 Glue the two pieces together to look like they are holding hands.

4 Wrap some masking tape around the back of the pin backing to make a better gluing surface. Glue the pin backing to the back of the joined puzzle pieces.

Wear your friends pin for Martin Luther King Day.

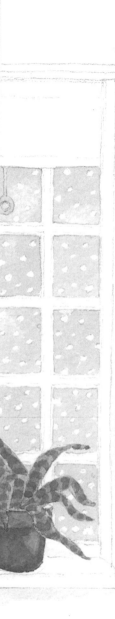

73)

Make some lacy snowflakes to
hang in your window.

Lace Snowflake

Here is what you need:

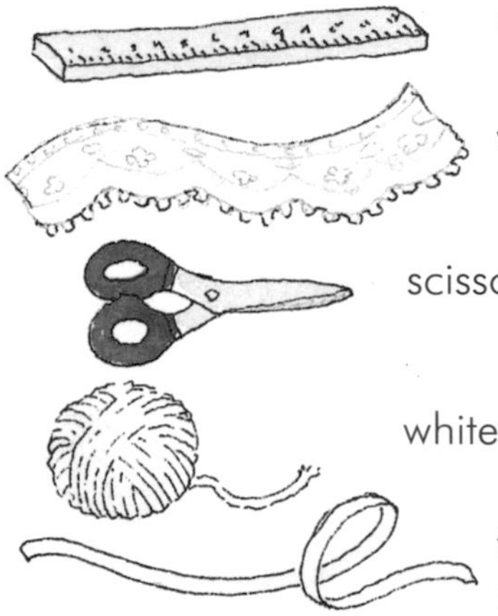

ruler

white lace

scissors

white yarn or string

thin white lace ribbon

white glue

water

margarine tub and craft stick for mixing

Styrofoam tray

Here is what you do:

1 Cut three 6-inch (15-cm)-long pieces of lace. Arrange the lace in a crisscross pattern like a wheel to make the six points of the snowflake.

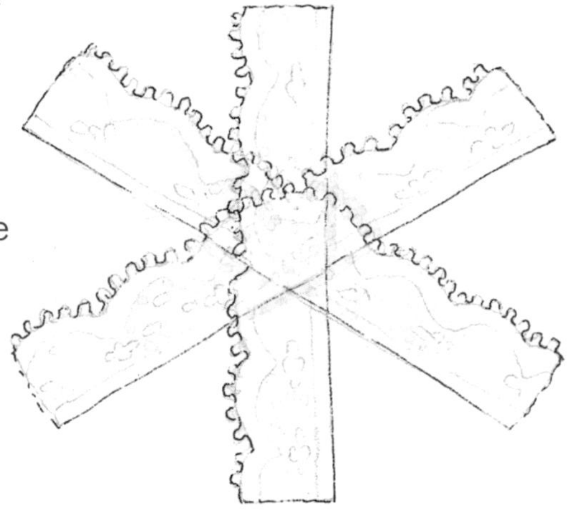

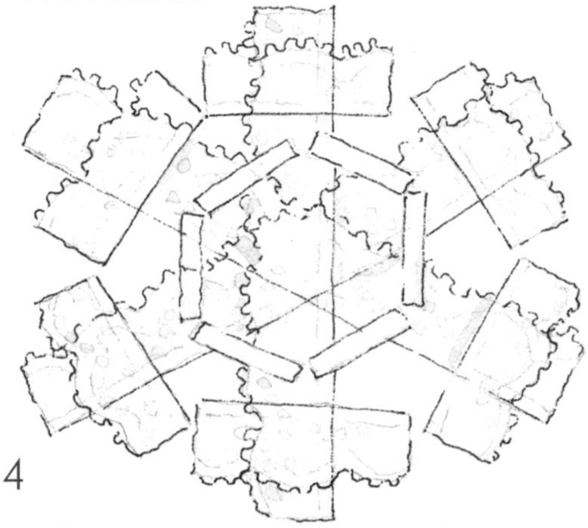

2 Cut smaller pieces of lace ribbon and yarn to put across the points of the snowflake. (Remember, each snowflake is different, and there are many possibilities. You will want to experiment with your own design.)

3 Mix one part of water to four parts of glue in the margarine tub, stirring with the craft stick.

4 Dip each piece of the snowflake into the watery glue and redo your snowflake design on the Styrofoam tray. Let the glue dry completely before peeling the hardened snowflake off the tray.

5 Cut a 2-foot (60-cm) length of string or yarn. Thread one end through an opening in the snowflake design and tie the two ends together to make a hanger. If your snowflake does not have an opening to thread the hanger through, punch a hole in one of the points and use that.

Make lots of different snowflakes to hang at different levels in the window.

Hungry Birds Puppet

Here is what you need:

newspaper to work on

6-inch (15-cm) paper plate

blue poster paint and a paintbrush

white glue

scissors

old knit glove

birdseed

two blue feather fluffs

cardboard toilet tissue tube

6-inch (15-cm) paper bowl

blue and orange felt scraps

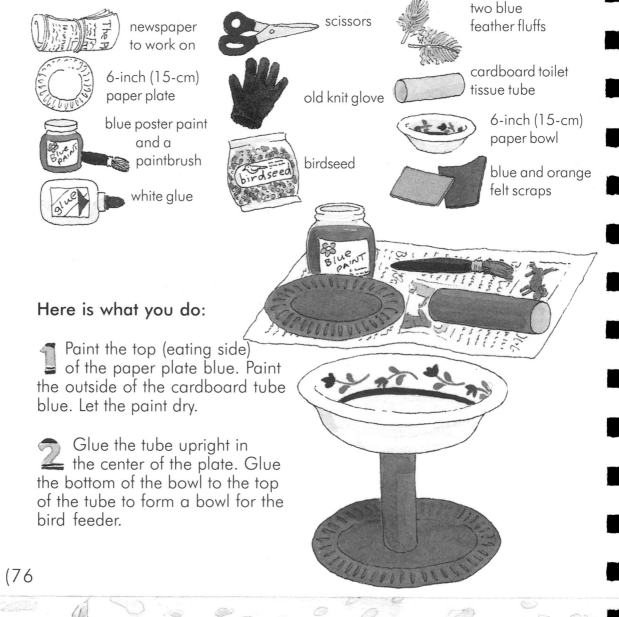

Here is what you do:

1 Paint the top (eating side) of the paper plate blue. Paint the outside of the cardboard tube blue. Let the paint dry.

2 Glue the tube upright in the center of the plate. Glue the bottom of the bowl to the top of the tube to form a bowl for the bird feeder.

3 Cut the two fingers next to the thumb out of the glove, leaving them attached at the base of each finger.

4 Cut two finger-size holes in the side of the bowl of the feeder. Put the glove fingers on your fingers and push them through each hole. Each finger will be a bird.

5 Cut a beak for each bird from the orange felt. Glue a beak on each bird on the side of the glove finger facing down into the feeder.

6 Cut eyes and wings for each bird from the blue felt and glue them in place.

7 Glue a fluff on the back of each bird for a tail.

8 Rub the bottom of the bowl of the feeder with glue, then sprinkle it with birdseed.

To use the bird feeder puppet, just slip a finger into each little bird and help them peck at the seeds in the bottom of the feeder.

77)

Pop-up Groundhog Puppet

Here is what you need:

- scissors
- adult-size brown sock
- 1-foot (30-cm) stick or dowel
- white glue
- 2½-inch (6-cm) Styrofoam ball
- small round oatmeal box
- two wiggle eyes
- string or yarn
- brown felt scraps
- fiberfill

Here is what you do:

1 Cut the bottom out of the oatmeal box. Slide the sock over the box, so that the cuff opening of the sock just fits around the edge of the box. The box will be the groundhog's hole.

2 Dip one end of the stick in glue, then push it into the Styrofoam ball. Push the ball through the box and into the toe of the sock, with the stick coming out of the bottom of the box. The ball will be the head of the groundhog. Tie a piece of string around the stick at the base of the Styrofoam ball to make the groundhog's neck.

3 Glue the two wiggle eyes on one side of the head. Cut ears and a nose from the brown felt and glue them in place.

4 Glue fiberfill around the top rim of the box for snow.

Push on the stick to pop your groundhog up out of the hole to see if he sees his shadow. If he sees it, pull on the stick to put him back in his hole for six more weeks of winter. "Oh, no!"

79)

Make this heart carrier for all of your valentine mail.

Heart Mail Carrier

Here is what you need:

scissors

red construction paper

pencil

white glue

large cereal box

red yarn

ruler

pretty rickrack, lace, or other trims

Here is what you do:

1 Cut the corner from the bottom of the box so that the side of the box is the same length as the bottom of the box. The open side of the triangle will be the top of your heart carrier.

2 Use a pencil to trace around one edge of the box on the red paper. Cut around the tracing, leaving an extra inch of paper on each side. Cut a second piece of paper the same size to cover the other edge of the triangle.

(80

3 Trace around the two sides of the point of the box. Turn the drawing into a heart by drawing two bumps on the top. Cut out a heart shape for each side of the box.

4 Cover the entire outside of the box with glue. Glue the side papers on each edge of the box, folding the extra paper down over the sides of the box. Trim off any extra paper.

5 Glue a heart to the front and the back of the box.

6 Decorate the heart with pretty trims. Use the trims to make your initials in the center of the heart on one side of the carrier.

7 Punch a hole in the top edge of each side of the heart box. Cut two 18-inch (46-cm) pieces of yarn. String a piece through each hole, then bring all four ends of the yarn up to the center above the heart and tie them to make a handle for the carrier.

This heart carrier looks pretty hanging up when not in use.

81)

Celebrate President's Day by making a hat like one that was worn by our first president . . .

George Washington Hat

Here is what you need:

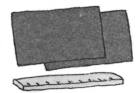 two pieces of 12- by 18-inch (30- by 46-cm) blue construction paper

ruler

scissors

masking tape

 white glue

plastic gallon milk jug for drying

foil cupcake wrapper

paintbrush

pencil

red ribbon

Here is what you do:

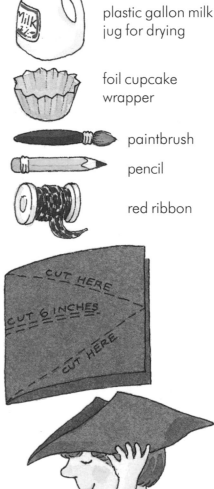
CUT HERE
CUT 6 INCHES
CUT HERE

1 Stack the two sheets of blue paper together. Fold the sheets of paper in half to make four layers of paper 9 by 12 inches (23 by 30 cm). Cut the corner off each side, making a 10-inch (25-cm)-long cut from each corner of the folded side to the top center of the paper. Starting at the center of the folded side, cut a 6-inch (15-cm) slit up the triangle shape.

2 Open the two layers of folded paper to get a hat. The slit in the hat should fit over the top of your head.

3 The two layers will need to be glued together. Put a small piece of masking tape at the end of each slit of each layer. Put the tape on the bottom side of the top layer and the top side of the bottom layer so that the tape will be in between the two layers and not show.

4 Glue the two hat layers together. Use the paintbrush to cover the inside completely with glue. Shape the damp hat over the milk jug to dry. The way you shape it on the jug will be the way it will stay once the glue hardens between the paper layers.

5 Flatten the foil cupcake wrapper to use for a medallion for the hat. Put a piece of masking tape on one side of the foil to create a better gluing surface. Cut a 12-inch (30-cm) piece of red ribbon. Fold the ribbon in half at an angle. Glue the folded end of the ribbon behind the foil so that the ends of the ribbon hang down. Put a piece of masking tape over the glued ribbon. Glue the medallion to one side of the hat.

Put on the hat and pretend you are sailing across the Delaware.

83)

Abraham Lincoln Mask

Here is what you need:

9-inch (23-cm) paper plate

scissors

newspaper to work on

stapler

black construction paper

white glue

black poster paint and a paintbrush

Here is what you do:

1 Cut the center out of the paper plate. Paint the entire back of the rim of the plate black for Abe's beard.

(84

2 Cut a 7- by 8-inch (18- by 20-cm) piece of black paper for the hat. Glue a 7-inch (18-cm) side of the paper to the edge of the black rim beard.

3 Cut a 2- by 12-inch (5- by 30-cm) strip of black paper for the rim of the hat. Glue the strip across the bottom of the hat.

4 Cut a strip of black paper to make a band for the back of the mask to hold it in place. Staple one end of the strip to one side of the mask behind the base of the hat. Fit the strip to your head, then staple the other end in place.

Do you know why Mr. Lincoln was such an important president?

85)

Freezing temperatures are needed to make this beautiful outdoor decoration.

Icy Sun Catcher

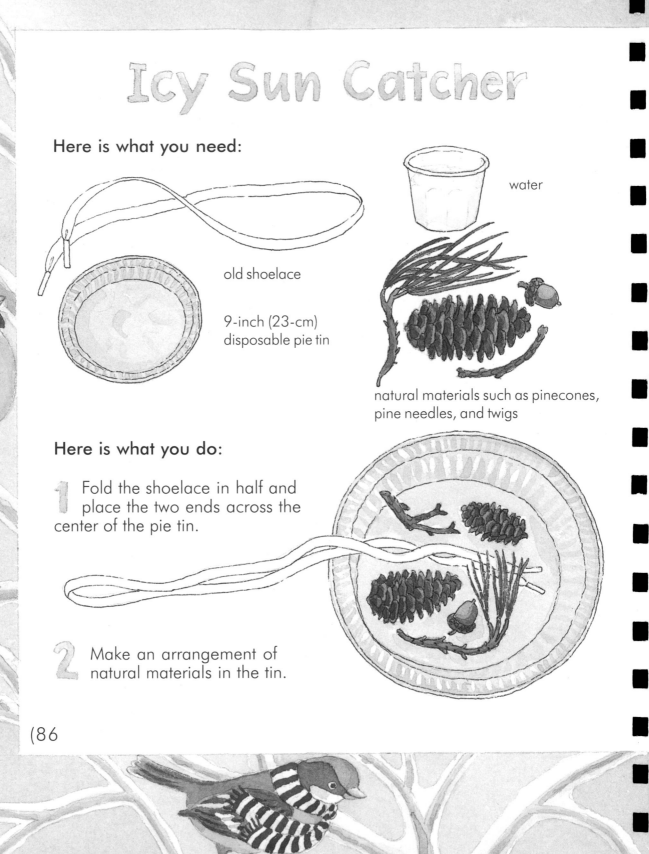

Here is what you need:

old shoelace

9-inch (23-cm) disposable pie tin

water

natural materials such as pinecones, pine needles, and twigs

Here is what you do:

1 Fold the shoelace in half and place the two ends across the center of the pie tin.

2 Make an arrangement of natural materials in the tin.

(86

3 Fill the tin with water and leave it outside to freeze.

4 When the water has frozen, remove the ice from the tin. Hang the ice circle from a tree in a sunny place so you can see it from your window.

This sun catcher will last only as long as the freezing weather does.

87)

February is National Dental Health month.

Happy Teeth Finger Puppets

Here is what you need:

markers

scissors

white glue

red construction paper

three 9-inch (23-cm) paper plates in skin color of choice

stapler

old white glove

yarn for hair

Here is what you do:

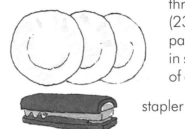

1 Draw an open mouth about 4 inches (10 cm) long and 2½ inches (6 cm) wide on the back of one paper plate. Cut the mouth area out.

2 Trace the open mouth on the back of a second paper plate and cut that mouth out too. The second plate will go under the first plate.

3 Use the markers to draw lips around the open mouth on the first plate. Also, draw eyes and a nose.

(88

4 Cut the thumb and the pinkie finger from the glove. Staple the two pieces hanging down from the top of the open mouth of the second plate so that they look like teeth.

5 Cut the remaining three fingers from the glove, leaving them attached at the base of the fingers. Staple the fingers sticking up like bottom teeth from the open mouth of the uncolored plate. Staple only one side of the base of the glove so that you can slip your fingers into the teeth to wiggle them.

6 Use the markers to draw a happy face on each tooth.

7 Staple the face plate to the plate with the teeth on the top and each side of the face.

8 Glue red paper over the top (eating side) of the third paper plate. Put the face plate over the paper-covered plate so that the red paper shows behind the mouth. Staple the plates together on the sides and the top.

9 Cut yarn bits for hair. Glue the yarn hair around the face.

Slip your fingers into the bottom teeth and have them remind everyone to brush their teeth so they will have happy teeth too.

Sprout a Pet

Here is what you need:

scissors

panty hose

hairpin

plastic food storage bag

birdseed

potting soil

two thumbtacks

water

Here is what you do:

1 Cut one leg off the panty hose. Fill the foot of the stocking leg with potting soil. Shake the soil-filled stocking gently to help the dirt settle, then add a little more to fill in the foot area.

2 Slide birdseed into the foot between the stocking and the dirt. Try to cover as much of the dirt with seed as you can.

3 Knot the stocking just above the foot to hold the dirt in place. Loop the excess stocking over and knot it to make a hanger for the dirt-filled foot.

(90

4 Put the two thumbtacks in the toe end of the foot for eyes. Slide one end of the hairpin through the top of the head and spread the two ends to look like antennae.

5 Moisten the seeds with water. A plant mister or spray bottle would be perfect for this job.

6 Slip the moistened critter into a plastic bag. Do not seal the bag. Place the bag in a dark area for a few days until the seeds start to sprout.

7 When the seeds have sprouted, hang your critter in a window and keep it moist.

You might want to design your own creature. You can use anything for details that will slip through the stocking material. Try using pipe cleaners or map pins to add details.

Crafts
to make
in the
Spring

For many, pussy willows are one of the first signs of spring.

Cotton Swab Pussy Willows

Here is what you need:

 cotton swabs (about 30)

two 12-inch (30-cm) brown pipe cleaners

pencil

one sheet of blue construction paper

stapler

piece of wallpaper

yarn

gray poster paint

scissors

white glue

Styrofoam tray for drying

Here is what you do:

1 Dip both ends of the cotton swabs in the gray paint. Put the swabs on the Styrofoam tray to dry.

2 Draw a vase on the back of the wallpaper. Make it a little less than half as tall as the piece of construction paper. Cut the vase out.

3 Cut each pipe cleaner in two so that one piece is slightly longer than the other piece.

(94

4 Glue the wallpaper vase onto the construction paper, putting the four pieces of pipe cleaner into the vase to look like stems.

5 Cut the gray ends off of each of the cotton swabs. For the pussy-willow buds, glue the fuzzy gray swab ends along the sides of each of the pipe-cleaner stems.

6 Cut a 24-inch (61-cm) piece of yarn. Fold the top inch (2.5 cm) of the picture back. Put the middle part of the yarn under the fold and staple the fold to hold it in place. Tie the two ends of the yarn together to make a hanger.

Meow!

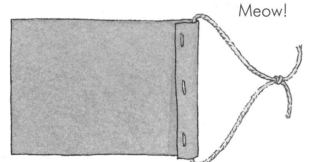

95)

Spotting a robin is a sure sign
of the coming of spring.

Robin Redbreast Door Hanging

Here is what you need:

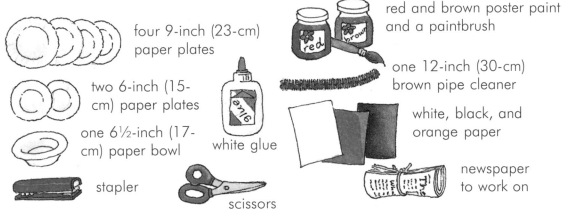

four 9-inch (23-cm)
paper plates

two 6-inch (15-
cm) paper plates

one 6½-inch (17-
cm) paper bowl

white glue

stapler

scissors

red and brown poster paint
and a paintbrush

one 12-inch (30-cm)
brown pipe cleaner

white, black, and
orange paper

newspaper
to work on

Here is what you do:

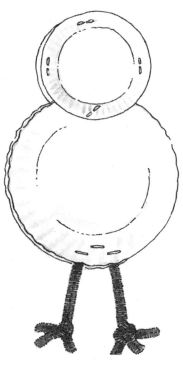

1 Fold the pipe cleaner in half. Cut a 1-inch (2.5-cm) piece off each end. To make a foot, bend the end of the pipe cleaner out and wrap the 1-inch piece around the foot to make toes. Repeat for the other foot. Staple two of the larger plates together with the bent pipe cleaner between them so that the legs hang down from the plate body.

2 Staple the two smaller plates together on one side. Slide the edge of one plate over the top front of the body and the other plate over the back. Staple the plates in place to make the head of the bird.

(96

3 Fold the two remaining plates in half. Staple one over each side of the body to form the wings.

4 Paint the entire bird brown. Paint the bottom of the bowl red.

FOLD

5 Staple the red bowl to the front of the bird to form the red breast. You can tell which is the front because the feet will be facing forward.

If your robin looks hungry, make it a worm from brown yarn or a pipe cleaner and glue it in the beak.

6 Cut eyes from the white and black paper and a beak from the orange paper. Glue them in place on the head of the bird.

97)

It is said that March comes in like a lion and goes out like a lamb.

Lion and Lamb Necklace

Here is what you need:

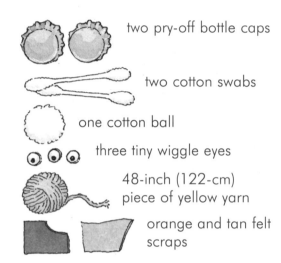

two pry-off bottle caps

two cotton swabs

one cotton ball

three tiny wiggle eyes

48-inch (122-cm) piece of yellow yarn

orange and tan felt scraps

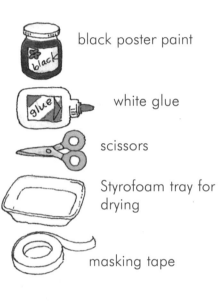

black poster paint

white glue

scissors

Styrofoam tray for drying

masking tape

Here is what you do:

1 Dip three of the four cotton swab ends in the black paint and let them dry on the Styrofoam tray. When they are dry, cut the tips off.

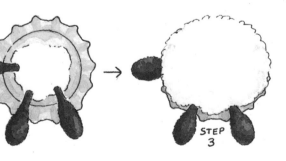

STEP 3

2 Fill one bottle cap with glue. Arrange one black swab sticking out off the side of the cap to form the head of the lamb. Put the other two sticking out of the bottom of the cap for the legs.

(98

3 Cover the cap with the cotton ball. If the cotton ball you are using is large, you may want to cut it so that it will fit in the cap neatly.

4 Glue a tiny wiggle eye on the head of the lamb.

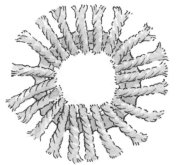

5 To make the lion, fill the second cap with glue. Cut about twenty 1-inch (2.5-cm) pieces of yellow yarn. Arrange them so that one end of each strand sticks out around the cap to make the mane of the lion.

6 Cut a circle of orange felt to glue in the cap. Cut tiny ears from the tan felt and glue them in place. Glue on two wiggle eyes.

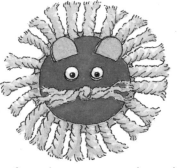

7 Put a piece of masking tape on the back of each cap to make a better gluing surface. Cut the yellow yarn to a good necklace length for you. Glue the two caps together, back to back, with the two ends of the yarn in between to form a necklace.

When the weather is cold and windy, wear the lion side of the necklace. When it is mild and springlike, wear the lamb side.

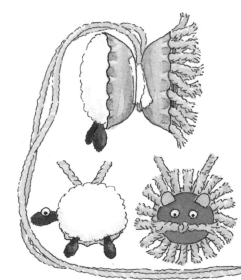

99)

The month of March is often very windy.

Huffing and Puffing Mr. Wind Puppet

Here is what you need:

four 9-inch (23-cm) paper plates

masking tape

white Styrofoam cup

light blue tissue paper

fiberfill

white glue

two wiggle eyes

liquid detergent bottle with pull-up cap

scissors

stapler

newspaper to work on

Here is what you do:

1 Staple two of the plates together to make one sturdier plate. Do the same with the other two plates. Hold the two doubled plates together with the eating sides facing each other and staple them together on each side. This will be the body of the wind puppet.

2 Glue fiberfill all over both sides of the puppet.

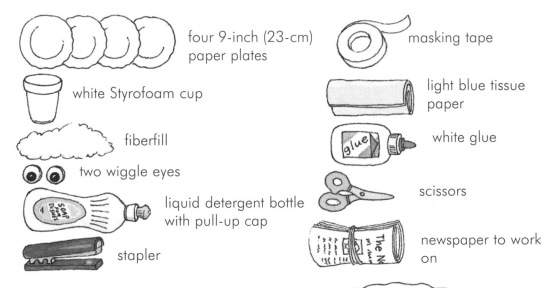

3 Cut the bottom out of the Styrofoam cup. Cut a 12-inch (30-cm) square of blue tissue paper and poke a large hole in the center of the square. Tuck the square into the open bottom of the cup so that the tissue sticks out. Tape the tissue to the inside of the cup, making sure that the hole you poked in the tissue is placed so that the cup is not blocked closed by the tissue. This will be the blowing mouth of the wind.

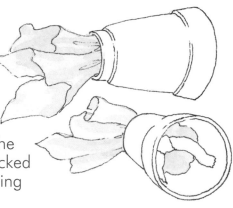

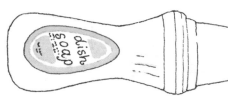

4 Pull open the top of the detergent bottle. Place the cup upside down over the top of the bottle and tape it in place. Slide the cup assembly, cup end first, between the plates of the wind body so that the tissue and the bottom edge of the cup stick out one side for the mouth. Add more staples to the top and bottom of the puppet to hold the bottle more securely, but be sure you can still slide your hand into the puppet.

5 Glue a wiggle eye on each side of the puppet behind the mouth.

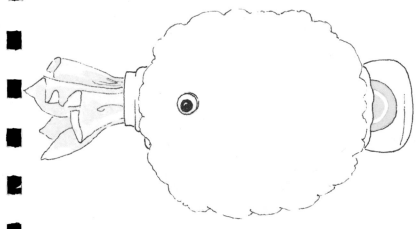

To make Mr. Wind huff and puff, just squeeze the bottle inside the puppet. You might want to cut some hats and leaves from the tissue paper for Mr. Wind to blow around.

101)

**Make this unusual wind sock
to sway in the spring breezes.**

Necktie Windsock

Here is what you need:

ten old neckties

various trims and rickracks

scissors

stapler

12- by 18-inch
(30- by 46-cm)
piece of
construction
paper

yarn

white glue

10 ✕

4"

Here is what you do:

1 Cut the ten neckties in half across the center of each tie. You will be using the thinner half of each tie for this project.

2 Fold 4 inches (10 cm) of the construction paper over lengthwise to make a strip. Trim off the extra paper along the bottom of the strip.

3 Open the folded strip and rub glue all over the inside of the paper. Arrange the cut ends of the ten neckties facedown and side by side along the edge of the folded paper. You will not have enough ties to go to the end of the strip. Fold the top of the gluey paper over the tie ends to hold them in place.

4 Carefully wrap the strip of paper around itself until you have a continuous circle of ties. Staple the strip to hold it in place. Let the glue dry.

5 Cut pieces of trim and rickrack to fit round the paper ring. Use glue to hold them in place.

6 Cut three 24-inch (61-cm) pieces of yarn to use for hangers. String the yarn pieces under the paper ring in three different places, then tie the ends together at the top.

Hang your wind sock outdoors for the wind to play with, but don't let it get wet!

Windy spring days are perfect for flying kites.

Hanger Kite Decoration

Here is what you need:

 wire coat hanger

old pair of brightly colored tights

black and white construction paper

red nail polish

bright-colored pom-pom

12-inch (30-cm) pipe cleaner or sparkle stem

three bow-shaped pieces of macaroni

scissors

 white glue

plastic lid for drying

Here is what you do:

1 Bend the wire hanger into the diamond shape of a kite. Cut one leg off the tights and use it to cover the hanger, starting at the bottom of the hanger. Knot the open end of the tights behind the hook of the hanger, making sure that the tights are pulled tight. Trim the excess material off the knot.

(104

2 Cut crossbars for the kite from the black paper and glue them to the kite. Cut eyes from the black and white paper and glue them to the kite. Glue the pom-pom below the eyes for a nose.

3 Paint the three macaroni pieces with nail polish. Let them dry on the plastic lid.

4 To make a tail for the kite, wrap the pipe cleaner around the center of a bow macaroni. Add two more bows about an inch (2.5 cm) apart. Poke a tiny hole through the fabric at the bottom of the kite. Push one end of the tail through the hole and twist it around the bottom of the hanger and then around itself to hold it in place.

Use the hook at the top of the hanger to hang your kite up for all to admire. Don't let it blow away!

105)

Celebrate St. Patrick's Day by making this giant shamrock to hang on your door.

Giant Shamrock

Here is what you need:

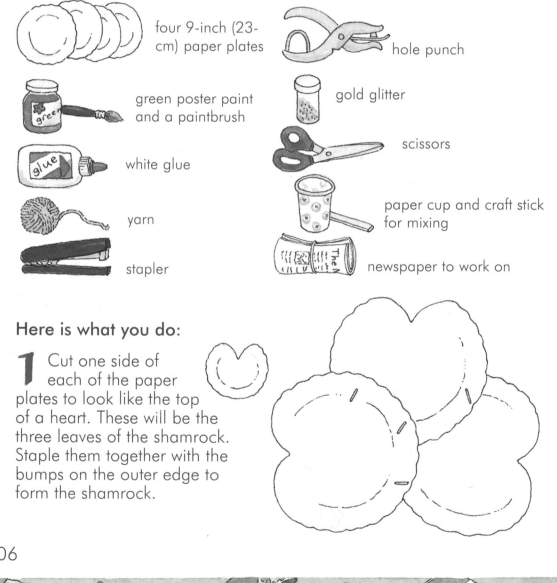

four 9-inch (23-cm) paper plates

hole punch

green poster paint and a paintbrush

gold glitter

white glue

scissors

yarn

paper cup and craft stick for mixing

stapler

newspaper to work on

Here is what you do:

1 Cut one side of each of the paper plates to look like the top of a heart. These will be the three leaves of the shamrock. Staple them together with the bumps on the outer edge to form the shamrock.

2 Cut a curved stem from the rim of the remaining paper plate. Staple it to the bottom of the shamrock.

3 Mix one part glue to two parts green paint in the paper cup. Paint the entire shamrock quickly, then sprinkle it with glitter while the glue and paint mixture is still wet.

4 Punch a hole in the top of the shamrock. Cut a 12-inch (30-cm) piece of yarn. Thread it through the hole and tie the two ends together to make a hanger.

This shamrock is too big to be carried off by the "little people."

107)

In the spring, many animals wake up from a long winter nap.

Wake-up Bear Bag Puppet

Here is what you need:

brown lunch bag

black, brown, and white construction paper

white glue

scissors

pencil

markers

Here is what you do:

1 Turn the bag upside down so that the bottom of the bag becomes the top of the bear puppet. Cut two eyes from white paper small enough to be hidden under the fold that was the bottom of the bag. Cut pupils from black paper to glue on each eye. Glue the eyes under the fold of the bag so they are hidden.

2 Cut two strips of black paper and fringe the edges to make eyelashes. Curl the paper lashes around a pencil to make them tip out slightly. Glue them to the bag bottom (that is now the head of the bear) over each eye.

2 -

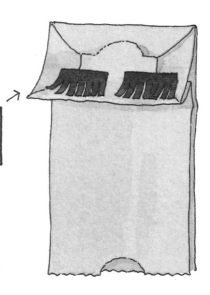

3 Cut ears, nose, and arms from the brown construction paper and glue them in place. Cut two nostrils from black paper to glue on the nose.

4 Use a marker to add to the bear any details you wish.

To wake up your sleeping bear, just slip your hand inside the bag and lift up the flap. Happy springtime, Bear!

109)

Crocuses are one of the first flowers to appear in the spring.

Crocus Dish Garden

Here is what you need:

 small margarine tub with lid

one 1½-inch (1-cm) Styrofoam ball

 Easter grass

scissors

 white glue

one yellow and three green 12-inch (30-cm) pipe cleaners

blue plastic wrap

green plastic tape

3 plastic spoons

pink or purple nail polish

masking tape

ribbon

Here is what you do:

1 Paint both sides of the bowls of the three spoons with nail polish. Place them to dry on the plastic lid from the margarine tub.

2 Cover the bottom of the inside of the margarine tub with masking tape. Cut the Styrofoam ball in half and cover the flat side of one half with a strip of masking tape. (Put the other half aside for another project). Glue the ball, taped side down, in the center of the margarine tub.

3 Fold the yellow pipe cleaner in half. Hold the three spoons, with the bowls curving in, around the folded pipe cleaner to look like petals around the stamen of the flower. Wrap green tape around the handles of the spoons to hold them in place and to make the stem of the flower.

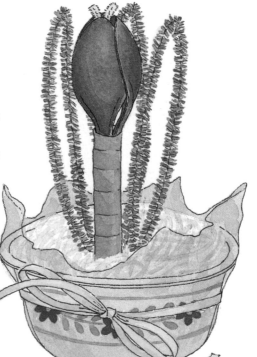

4 Press the bottom of the flower into the center of the Styrofoam ball in the margarine tub. Fold each of the three green pipe cleaners in half and stick the ends in the Styrofoam around the base of the flower to make leaves.

5 Rub glue all over the Styrofoam around the flower and cover it with Easter grass. Use ribbon to tie a square of blue plastic wrap around the margarine tub.

You can enjoy this pretty symbol of spring any time of the year.

111)

Many people find the sound of spring rain very soothing.

Pitter-patter Rain Stick

Here is what you need:

long cardboard tube from gift wrap

uncooked rice

aluminum foil

spring stickers

Here is what you do:

1 Tear off a strip of aluminum foil about one and a half times as long as the cardboard tube. Squeeze the sides of the foil together to make a long snakelike strip.

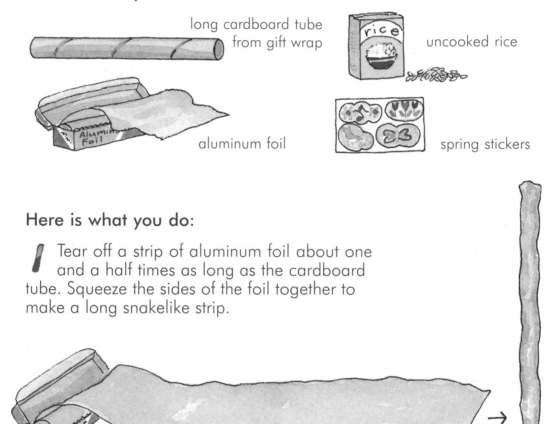

2 Tear off a second strip of foil that is 6 inches (15 cm) longer than the cardboard tube. Wrap the foil around the tube so that there are about 3 extra inches (8 cm) sticking out from each end of the tube. Fold the extra foil over at one end of the tube to close that end.

3 Bend the long strip of foil into a zigzag shape so that it will fit inside the tube. Slide it in. Drop in a handful of rice. Seal the open end of the tube by folding over the extra foil. Be sure you haven't left anyplace where the rice could fall out!

4 Decorate the rain stick with pretty spring stickers.

To hear the pleasing sound of falling rain just tip the stick, hold it still, and listen.

In many places, springtime means the arrival of lots of pretty birds.

Spring Bird Mask

Here is what you need:

two 9-inch (23-cm) paper plates

cardboard paper towel tube

poster paints and a paintbrush

newspaper to work on

two white or light-colored oval-shaped shoulder pads

craft feathers

white glue

scissors

Styrofoam tray for drying

Here is what you do:

1 Glue the two plates together to make them stronger. Cut two eyeholes from the plate. Paint the bottom of the plate in the color of your choice. You can make your mask to look like a real bird or design a colorful bird of your own.

2 Paint both sides of both shoulder pads to make the beak. Let them dry on the Styrofoam tray.

3 Cut a 2½-inch (6-cm) slit in the plate below the eyes. Stack the two shoulder pads, one on top of the other, and pull the pointed ends of one side through the slit so that the pads stick out to form the beak of the bird.

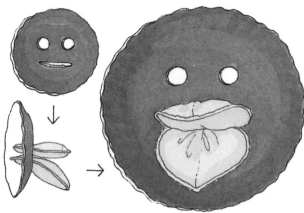

4 Glue craft feathers above the eyes of the bird to make a crest.

5 Paint the cardboard tube a bright color. Cut a 2-inch (5-cm) slit on each side of one end of the tube. Slide the bottom of the bird head into the slits so you have a holder for the bird mask.

Make masks for your friends, and you could have a whole flock of colorful birds this spring!

Growing Flower

Here is what you need:

 old tube of lipstick

 stapler

6-inch (15-cm) red and 6-inch green pipe cleaner

scissors

craft stick

brown construction paper

Here is what you do:

1 Turn the lipstick all the way up in the tube. Use the craft stick to scrape the lipstick off level with the inner case.

2 Cut a 4-inch (10-cm) piece of green pipe cleaner for the flower stem. Wrap the remaining piece around the upper part of the stem to make leaves. Shape a flower from the red pipe cleaner. Attach it to the top of the stem.

(116

3 Push the bottom of the flower stem down into the remaining lipstick in the tube.

4 Cut the front and the back of a flowerpot from the brown paper. Make the pot as tall as the lipstick tube. Staple the two sides of the front and the back of the pot together with the tube between them.

To make the flower grow, just turn the outer case of the lipstick tube. This flower grows without the rain!

TURN LIPSTICK TUBE HERE

117)

Get ready to help with the "spring cleaning."

Here is what you need:

roll of white paper towels

ribbon

stapler

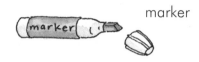

marker

Here is what you do:

1 Tear off a strip of three paper towels, leaving them attached. Make a flat pile of six strips of three paper towels each.

2 Cut a piece of ribbon long enough for the person using the apron to tie around his or her waist.

Spring Cleaning Apron
Tear off paper towels as needed

3 Fold the pile of towels in half over the center of the ribbon to make an apron. Staple the towels together on each side to hold them in place.

4 Use the marker to write "Spring Cleaning Apron" and "Tear off paper towels as needed."

This handy apron will keep the wearer supplied with paper towels for a whole day of spring cleaning.

119)

In some places, children dance around the "Maypole" to celebrate the first day of May.

Maypole Hat

Here is what you need:

- cardboard paper-towel tube
- pencil
- paper bowl
- ribbon in several different colors
- white glue
- newspaper to work on
- hole punch
- scissors
- green poster paint and a paintbrush
- artificial flowers

Here is what you do:

1 Trace around the end of the paper-towel tube on the center of the bottom of the bowl. Cut the traced circle out of the bowl.

2 Cut several 1-inch (2.5-cm)-deep slits around one end of the tube. Slip the cut end of the tube into the hole on the bottom of the bowl. Spread the slits out and glue them to the inside of the bowl to hold the tube in place. This will be the Maypole.

3 Paint the Maypole green and let it dry.

4 Cut eight or more 18-inch (46-cm) pieces of ribbon. Rub glue around the inside of the top of the tube. Press the ends of each ribbon down into the glue in the top of the tube. Arrange the ribbons so that they hang down around the tube pole. Dip the ends of some artificial flowers in glue and tuck them in the top of the pole.

5 Punch a hole on each side of the bowl. Tie the end of a 24-inch (61-cm) piece of ribbon through each hole so that the Maypole can be tied on to wear as a hat.

Put on the hat, twirl around, and pretend you are a Maypole!

Springtime means lots of creeping, crawling things!

Sock Caterpillar

Here is what you need:

scissors

child-size white sock

two wiggle eyes

old socks for stuffing

white glue

cardboard paper-towel or toilet-tissue tube

6-inch (15-cm) green pipe cleaner or sparkle stem

green and yellow poster paint and a paintbrush

Styrofoam tray for drying

Here is what you do:

1 Stuff the small sock to make a caterpillar body. Tuck the open end of the sock down into itself on one side to close the sock and form a mouth for the caterpillar.

2 Paint the entire caterpillar body yellow.

3 Cut four 1-inch (2.5-cm)-wide rings from the cardboard tube. Paint the rings green.

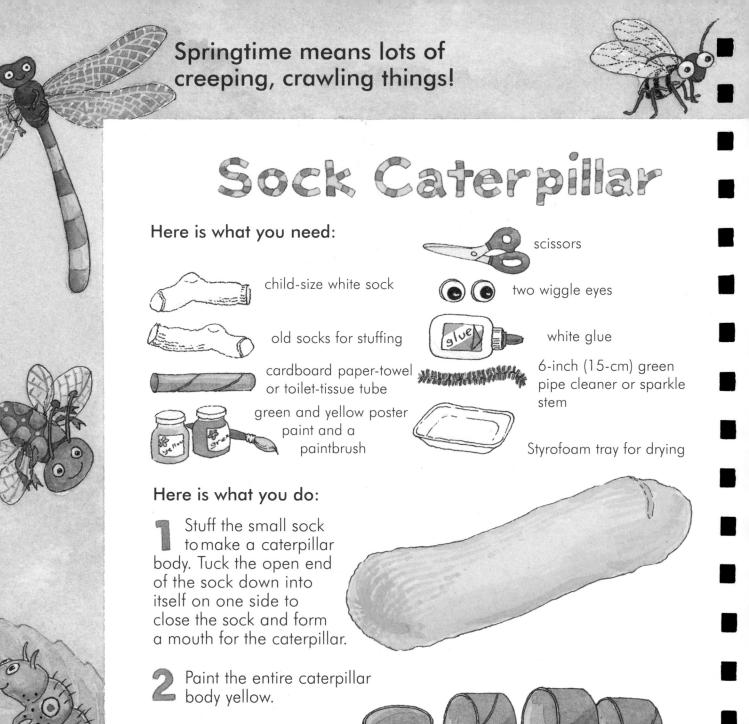

4 Slide the rings over the body of the caterpillar and arrange them so they are evenly spaced to give the caterpillar stripes. Glue the rings in place.

5 Cut a 4-inch (10-cm) piece of pipe cleaner. Thread one end in one side of the top of the caterpillar head and out the other to make the antennae. Bend the end of each antenna to the side.

6 Glue two wiggle eyes to the front of the caterpillar above the mouth.

You might want to make your creepy, crawly caterpillar in a different combination of colors.

Design your own butterfly with this project.

Plastic Bag Butterfly

Here is what you need:

wooden clamp clothespin

6-inch (15-cm) pipe cleaner

2 wiggle eyes

yellow poster paint and a paintbrush

white glue

gallon-size plastic bag

stapler

colorful pieces of tissue paper

mylar from deflated balloons

confetti

sticky-back magnet

Styrofoam tray for drying

Here is what you do:

1 Paint the clothespin yellow and let it dry.

2 Fill the plastic bag lightly with colorful bits of tissue paper, confetti, and mylar. Fold the open end of the bag over and staple along the fold to hold it shut.

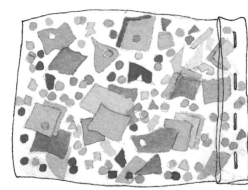

3 Gather the bag together at the center, and slide it in between the clamps of the clothespin.

4 Shape the ends of the pipe cleaner into antennae. Glue the center of the pipe cleaner between the clamps of the clothespin.

5 Press a piece of sticky-back magnet on the back of the butterfly.

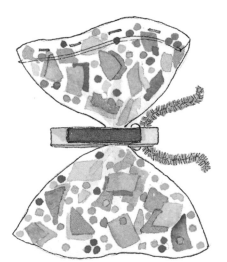

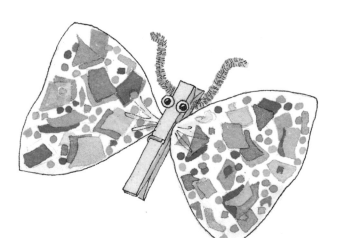

Surprise someone you know by sticking a beautiful spring butterfly to their refrigerator!

125)

Make a vase to hold some sweet-smelling spring flowers.

Vase for Spring Flowers

Here is what you need:

 16-ounce (454-gram) can, empty, with the top cut off

 9-ounce (255-gram) plastic cup to fit exactly inside the can

 colorful woman's sock

 masking tape

ribbons and trims

 felt in a color that looks nice with the sock

white glue

scissors

ballpoint pen

Here is what you do:

1 Cut the foot off the sock. Use the cuff of the sock to cover the can. Push the cup down into the can to hold the sock in place at the top.

2 Use masking tape to tape the bottom of the sock flat against the bottom of the can.

(126

3 Trace around the bottom of the can on the felt. Cut the felt circle out and glue it over the taped bottom of the can.

4 Use lace, ribbon, or other trims to decorate the sock-covered can.

You might want to make the "bottle bottom flowers" on page 128 to put in your vase when real flowers aren't available.

127)

If you just can't wait for the spring flowers to bloom, try making some of these flowers.

Bottle Bottom Flowers

Here is what you need:

 16-ounce (454-milliliter) plastic soda bottle

yellow and green construction paper

green plastic straw

scissors

clear packing tape

colored glue

hole punch

Here is what you do:

1 Have an adult help you cut the bottom off of the plastic soda bottle about 1 inch (2.5 cm) up from the bottom. This will give you a very nice flower shape.

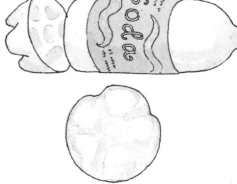

2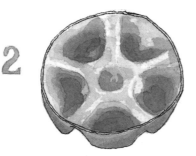

Color the plastic flower by covering the inside of the bottle bottom with colored glue. Let the glue dry completely before continuing. This could take up to two days.

(128

3 To make the front and back cover for the album, cut four squares from remaining sides of the box. They should be the same size as your frame pages. Glue two squares together, print side out, for the front of the book. Do the same with the other two squares to make the back cover of the book. Use paper clips to hold the cardboard together while the glue dries.

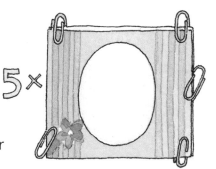

4 Stack the covers and album pages together in the order you want them to be. Punch two holes in the left side of the cover page. Use a pencil to mark where to punch the holes in the next page. Keep doing this until all the pages have holes.

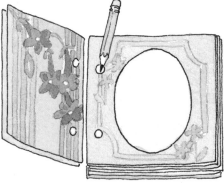

5 Use ribbon to tie two pages together. Tie the ribbon in a bow on the front side of the album.

Make this gift extra special by slipping a picture of you into the frame on the first page.

133)

Crafts
to make
in the
Summer

Talking Sun Puppet

Here is what you need:

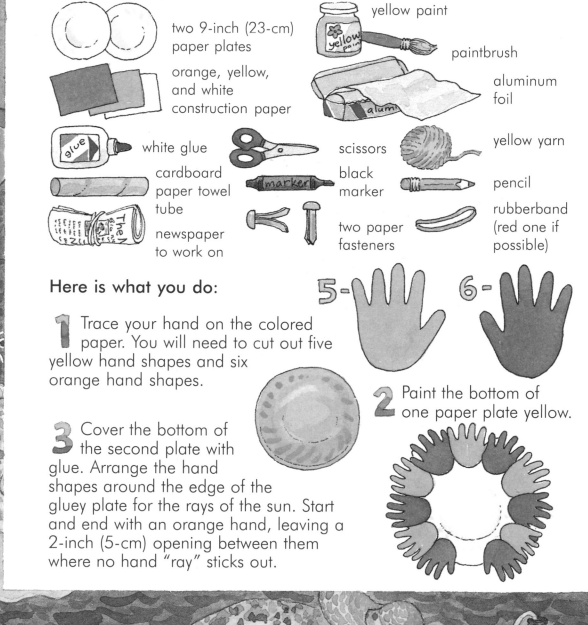

- two 9-inch (23-cm) paper plates
- orange, yellow, and white construction paper
- white glue
- cardboard paper towel tube
- newspaper to work on
- yellow paint
- paintbrush
- aluminum foil
- scissors
- black marker
- two paper fasteners
- yellow yarn
- pencil
- rubberband (red one if possible)

Here is what you do:

1 Trace your hand on the colored paper. You will need to cut out five yellow hand shapes and six orange hand shapes.

2 Paint the bottom of one paper plate yellow.

3 Cover the bottom of the second plate with glue. Arrange the hand shapes around the edge of the gluey plate for the rays of the sun. Start and end with an orange hand, leaving a 2-inch (5-cm) opening between them where no hand "ray" sticks out.

4 Set the top of the painted plate over the gluey plate so that you have a yellow sun with rays all around it. The opening will be the bottom.

5 To make the mouth, push the two paper fasteners into the sun above the opening and about 3 inches (8 cm) apart. Hook an end of the rubberband over each fastener. Open the fasteners on the back of the sun to secure them.

6 Cut two eyes from the white paper. Use the black marker to draw a pupil on each eye. Glue the eyes to the face of the sun.

7 Cover the cardboard tube with aluminum foil. Fold the extra foil down into the two ends of the tube. Cut a 2-inch (5-cm) slit on each side of the opening at one end of the tube. Slide the bottom edge of the sun into the slit.

8 Tie one end of a 24-inch (61-cm) length of yellow yarn to the bottom of the rubberband mouth. Drop the yarn down through the tube holder so that it hangs out. To make the sun puppet look like it is talking, just pull on the end of the yarn.

What does your sun want to say?

**Make this fan to cool you off
on those hot summer days.**

Plate Fan

Here is what you need:

 two 9-inch (23 cm) paper plates

markers in several bright colors

tissue paper in several bright colors

plastic tub for mixing

water

white glue

scissors

paintbrush

tongue depressor

yarn

newspaper to work on

Here is what you do:

1 Use the markers to make areas of bright color on the front of one plate and the back of the other.

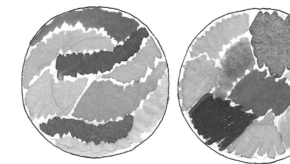

2 Glue the two plates together with the colors showing on the outside and the end of the tongue depressor forming a handle between them.

3 Cut flowers from different colored tissue paper. Cut a center for each flower from a contrasting color. Cut some green tissue leaves.

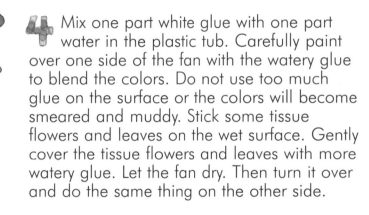

4 Mix one part white glue with one part water in the plastic tub. Carefully paint over one side of the fan with the watery glue to blend the colors. Do not use too much glue on the surface or the colors will become smeared and muddy. Stick some tissue flowers and leaves on the wet surface. Gently cover the tissue flowers and leaves with more watery glue. Let the fan dry. Then turn it over and do the same thing on the other side.

5 Cover the handle with glue, then wrap it in yarn.

What a pretty way to stir up a breeze!

This little mouse will keep your sunglasses safe when you're not using them.

Mouse Sunglasses Case

Here is what you need:

old necktie

plastic wrap

yarn

scissors

two large and one medium-size pom-poms

white glue

sticky Velcro dots fastener

clamp clothespins

two wiggle eyes

Here is what you do:

1 Cut a 9-inch (23-cm) long piece using the wide end of the necktie. (Don't include the point of the tie when you measure.) Carefully cut the tag off the back of the tie. If the front of the tie is sewn to the back of the tie, cut the threads. If the seam of the tie is unraveling, glue it back together. Use a small amount of glue so that you do not stain the fabric. Slip some plastic wrap behind the seam to keep the glue from soaking through the front of the tie.

9"

2 Fold the cut opening of the tie inside itself and glue it together. Use clamp clothespins to hold the seam in place until the glue has dried.

(140

3 Stick a Velcro dot on the inside point of the tie. Fold the point over to close the top. Put the other dot on the tie in a position so that the Velcro dots will meet when the case is closed.

4 Turn the case into a mouse by gluing a large pom-pom ear on each side of the top of the case above the closed point. Glue two wiggle eyes below the ears. Cut two, 3-inch (8-cm) long pieces of yarn. Knot the yarn in the middle, then fray the ends to look like whiskers. Glue the whiskers on the tip of the point with a pom-pom nose glued over the knot in the center.

You might want to make your sunglasses case to look like a different animal. Use your own ideas to make your favorite critter.

141)

Collect farewell messages from your school friends and hello messages from your new camp friends.

Greeting Card Autograph Book

Here is what you need:

 ten or more old greeting cards

hole punch

scissors

 cereal box cardboard

 marker

 pencil

ribbon

Here is what you do:

1 Draw a simple shape on the box cardboard to use as a pattern for the pages of your book. A heart, circle, or flower would work well. The shape should be small enough to fit on the greeting cards. Cut the shape out.

2 Trace the shape on the front of the card you wish to use for a cover for the book. Cut the shape out.

(142

3 Trace the shape on the back of the picture on the front of all the other greeting cards. The back will be the front of the page in your book so that people can write a message that will show well. The greeting card pictures will appear across from each page when the book is tied together. Cut all the shapes out.

4 Stack all the pages together with the cover on the front. Punch two holes through the left edge of the stacked pages. Use the ribbon to tie the pages together loosely so that they will turn easily.

Write on the front of the book with a marker. You could write "Fourth Grade" or the name of your camp or just "My Friends" and the year. Think about making another book next year so that you will someday have a collection to help you remember those special times in your life.

143)

June, and the start of summer, is the most popular time for weddings.

Play Wedding Veil

Here is what you need:

white tissue paper

tissue or crepe paper in your choice of colors

old pair of pantyhose

scissors

stapler

Here is what you do:

1 Cut the waistband off of the pantyhose. This will be the headband for the veil.

2 Pinch the top of the long side of the sheet of white tissue paper together to make the veil. Spread it out to fit and staple it along one half of the headband. The ends of the staples should be on the outside of the veil so that they will not catch your hair if they do not close completely.

(144

3 Cut 3-inch (8-cm) circles from the colored tissue paper to make flowers. Cut 2-inch (5-cm) squares of tissue to make a center for each flower. Place a square in the center of each circle and pinch the center together to form a flower. Staple the flowers all the way around the headband (half of them will be on top of the white tissue veil). Again, make sure that the staple closes on the outside of the headband.

Here comes the bride!

145)

Photo Key Chain

Here is what you need:

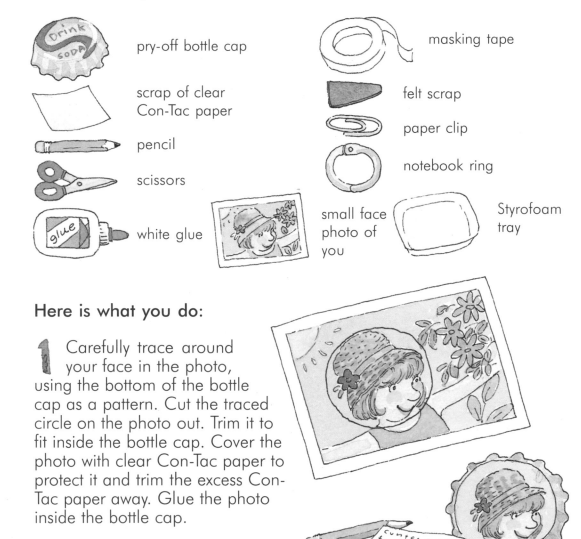

- pry-off bottle cap
- scrap of clear Con-Tac paper
- pencil
- scissors
- white glue
- masking tape
- felt scrap
- paper clip
- notebook ring
- small face photo of you
- Styrofoam tray

Here is what you do:

1 Carefully trace around your face in the photo, using the bottom of the bottle cap as a pattern. Cut the traced circle on the photo out. Trim it to fit inside the bottle cap. Cover the photo with clear Con-Tac paper to protect it and trim the excess Con-Tac paper away. Glue the photo inside the bottle cap.

(146

2 Cover the back of the bottle cap with masking tape. Glue a paper clip to the back of the cap with the end sticking up over the top of the photo in front. Cover the bottom of the paper clip with masking tape. Cut a circle of felt to cover the back of the cap. Glue it on the back of the cap to cover the bottom of the paper clip. Let the project dry on a Styrofoam tray.

3 Open the notebook ring and slip one end through the paper clip. Close the notebook ring.

What a nice surprise for your dad!

147)

Show your patriotic spirit by wearing this Uncle Sam mask on the Fourth of July.

Uncle Sam Mask

Here is what you need:

- 9-inch (23-cm) paper plate
- red, white, and blue construction paper
- sticker stars
- fiberfill
- white glue
- scissors
- stapler

Here is what you do:

1 Cut the center out of the paper plate, so that you are left with just the rim.

TAPE

2 Cut an 8-inch by 9-inch (20- by 23-cm) piece of blue construction paper for the hat. Cut a 2-inch by 12-inch (5- by 30-cm) blue rectangle for the brim of the hat. Glue the brim across the bottom of one of the shorter sides of the hat piece.

3 Cut a band and stripes for the hat from the red and white paper. Arrange them in a way you like, then glue them in place. Finish the hat by decorating it with sticker stars.

4 Glue a fiberfill beard around half of the plate rim. Staple the hat to the plate rim above the beard.

BACKSIDE

5 Cut a paper band that will be just long enough to fit around your head when attached to each side of the plate rim behind the hat. Staple the band to the plate rim.

Have a glorious Fourth of July!

149)

This happy little firecracker will be around to share more than one Fourth of July with you.

Firecracker Finger Puppet

Here is what you need:

 reddish color coin wrapper

 two wiggle eyes

★ ★ sticker stars

 red marker

small bubble wrap

two 12-inch (30-cm) sparkle stems

small red pom-pom

 scissors

white glue

Here is what you do:

1 Cut the two sparkle stems in half. Glue the ends of the four pieces inside one end of the coin wrapper. Let the glue dry, then fan the stems out to look like an exploding firecracker.

2 Glue the two wiggle eyes on one side of the wrapper, just below the stems. Glue on a pom-pom nose below the eyes. Use the marker to give the firecracker a smile.

3 Decorate the wrapper with sticker stars.

4 Cut two or three bubbles from small bubble wrap and slip them inside the firecracker. Pop the bubbles to make the firecracker "explode." Have lots of extra bubbles ready for "reloading."

Slip the firecracker over your finger and go wish someone a happy Fourth of July!

Bubble blowing is a favorite warm-weather activity.

Bubble Machine

Here is what you need:

8 oz. (227g) plastic margarine tub with lid

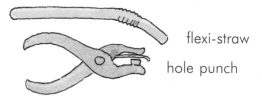
flexi-straw

hole punch

black permanent marker

self-stick stickers

liquid dish soap or detergent

Here is what you do:

1 Punch a hole in the top edge of the plastic margarine tub. Punch another hole in the edge of its lid. Replace the lid, positioning the hole in the lid on the opposite side from the hole in the tub.

2 Write "The Bubble Machine" on the top of the lid with the marker.

3 Decorate around the tub with stickers.

4 Slide the straw into the hole in the side of the tub, bent end first.

5 To use the bubble machine, open the lid and put in a squirt of liquid dish soap. Fill the tub halfway full with water. Put the lid on and blow through the straw. You will be rewarded with a cascade of bubbles pouring out through the hole in the lid.

Try blowing very slowly to see how big a bubble you can make.

Summertime means lots of picnics. Make this sit-upon to use when the ground is damp.

Sit-Upon

Here is what you need:

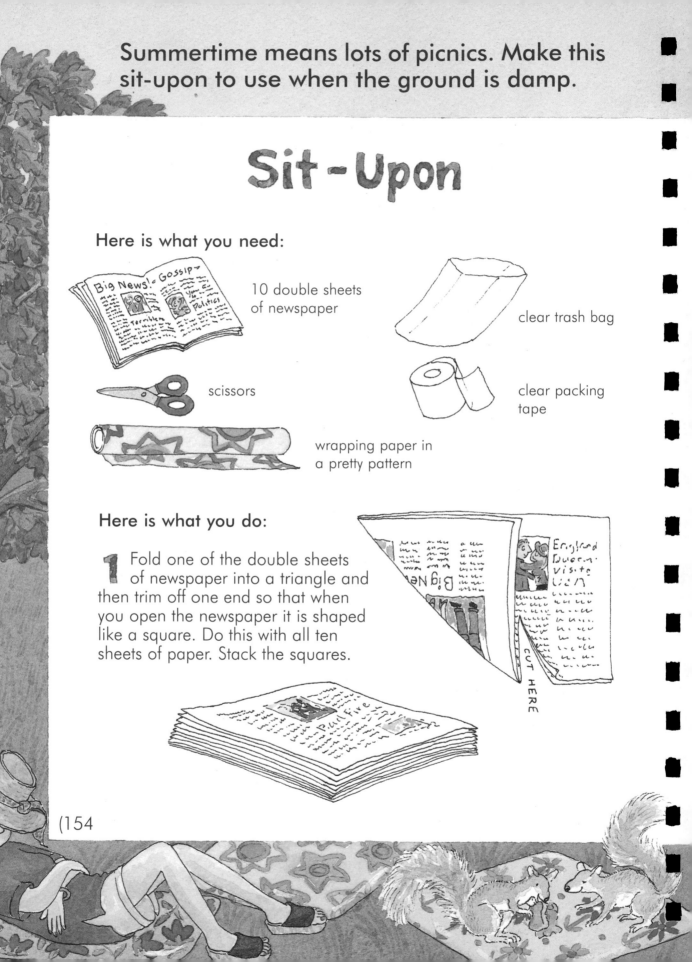

10 double sheets of newspaper

clear trash bag

scissors

clear packing tape

wrapping paper in a pretty pattern

Here is what you do:

1 Fold one of the double sheets of newspaper into a triangle and then trim off one end so that when you open the newspaper it is shaped like a square. Do this with all ten sheets of paper. Stack the squares.

CUT HERE

2 Cover the stack of newspaper with wrapping paper, wrapping the stack of squares in the paper and taping the ends just as you would a present. This will be your mat to sit on.

3 Put the mat into one corner of the bottom of the clear trash bag. Trim the top part of the bag off about 6 inches (15 cm) above the mat. Fold the excess bag at the top and one side of the mat over to make the bag cover the square exactly. Use packing tape to hold the bag in place and seal any open seams to make it waterproof.

A sit-upon is just what you need for picnics and camping trips.

Swimming Fish Box

Here is what you need:

box with acetate cover, such as the type stationery comes in

craft foam or flat packing foam

bubble wrap

markers

stapler

scissors

facial tissue

Here is what you do:

1 Use the markers to color an ocean scene on the bottom of the box.

marker
marker

(156

2 Cut a piece of bubble wrap to cover the bottom and sides of the inside box. Staple the bubble wrap in place over the ocean scene.

3 Cut 1-inch (2.5-cm) long fish from the craft foam. If you do not have two or three different colors of foam, you may want to add some color or detail with the markers. Make at least ten fish.

4 Put the fish inside the box and put the lid on. To make the fish swim around inside the box, rub the plastic lid with a facial tissue. Rubbing your fingers across the lid can work too. The static electricity that you create causes the fish to move around the ocean scene.

You might want to add some other sea creatures to your ocean scene. Maybe a wavy eel or sea turtle?

Some people do not like to touch fish, but this fish is fun to feel.

Squishy Fish

Here is what you need:

construction paper in two colors

black and white construction paper

rick-rack or other trim

yarn

quart-size, zip-to-close plastic bag

pencil

sequins

hair gel, clear or colored

cereal box cardboard

scissors

masking tape

white glue

stapler

Here is what you do:

1 Squeeze enough hair gel into the bag to fill it when it is lying flat. Add lots of pretty sequins to the gel. Zip the bag almost completely shut, then work any air bubbles in the gel up to the opening and out of the bag.

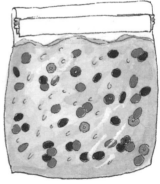

2 Completely seal the bag. Fold the sealed end over and tape it down with masking tape.

3 Fold a piece of 9-inch by 12-inch (23- by 30-cm) construction paper in half to get a piece of paper that is 6 by 9 inches (15- by 23-cm).

(158

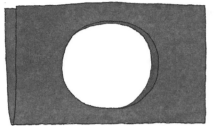

4 Sketch the outline of a fish body without the tail on the folded paper. A circle is fine. Make sure the fish is smaller than the gel bag. Cut the fish body out of the center of the paper, through both layers.

5 Holding the folded paper with the opening at the top, place the gel bag between the folds, with the taped top of the bag at the top open end of the paper. Staple the folded paper shut through the portion of the gel bag above the opening only. (If you staple through the gel bag itself, you will cause it to leak.) Staple the sides of the paper fold shut, also.

6 Cut a 1- by 9-inch (2.5- by 23-cm) strip of cardboard. Staple it across the back of the top opening of the paper for support.

7 Cut a paper tail for the fish and glue it on one side of the fish body.

8 Put a small piece of masking tape on the other end of the fish body. Make an eye for the fish using the black and white construction paper. Stick the eye on the masking tape on the fish body.

9 Cut the rick-rack or trim to glue around the edges of the paper to cover the staples.

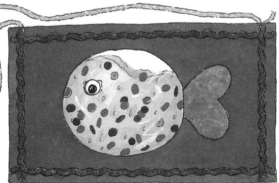

10 Cut a hanger for the fish from yarn and staple an end to each side of the cardboard support at the back of the project.

When you are not squishing your fish, you can hang it in a sunny window for the light to shine through.

159)

These little float toys are great for playing in the water on hot summer days.

Cork Float Toys

Here is what you need:

 cork

 two thumbtacks

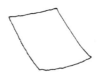 white paper

 clear packing tape

scissors

markers

Here is what you do:

1 Ask an adult to cut a deep ½-inch (1-cm) long slit in the side of the cork.

2 On the white paper, draw a small picture of something you might find in the water. You could draw some sort of boat or a water animal like a duck. Draw a tab on the bottom of the picture just wide enough to slip into the slit of the cork.

(160

3 Cut out the picture, with the tab. Cover both sides of the picture with clear packing tape to make it waterproof. Cut the picture out again, this time out of the clear tape.

4 Put the picture tab into the slit in the cork.

5 Put a thumbtack on each side of the bottom of the cork below the picture to help keep the cork balanced in the water. (You may need to adjust the thumbtacks to get your toy to float in an upright position.)

How about making a fleet of floating toys and having a race?

Jar Water Carafe and Glass

Here is what you need:

two jars, a small one with
a rim that will just fit inside a
larger one (a large baby food jar
and a 25-ounce-size applesauce
jar seem to work well together)

nail polish

Here is what you do:

1 Find a small jar with a
rim that just fits inside the
larger jar. The small jar will be
the water glass and the larger
jar will be the water holder.
Wash the jars in hot, soapy
water to clean them, and
remove the labels completely.

(162

2 Use nail polish to decorate the outside of the large jar.

Fill the large jar with ice water before you go to bed and put the smaller jar over the large jar for a top. If you wake up in the night feeling hot and thirsty, just take the top jar off the water and use it for a glass. Pour yourself a nice cool drink!

163)

Long ago girls and women wore big sunbonnets to protect themselves from the hot summer sun.

Sunbonnet Girl Door Hanging

Here is what you need:

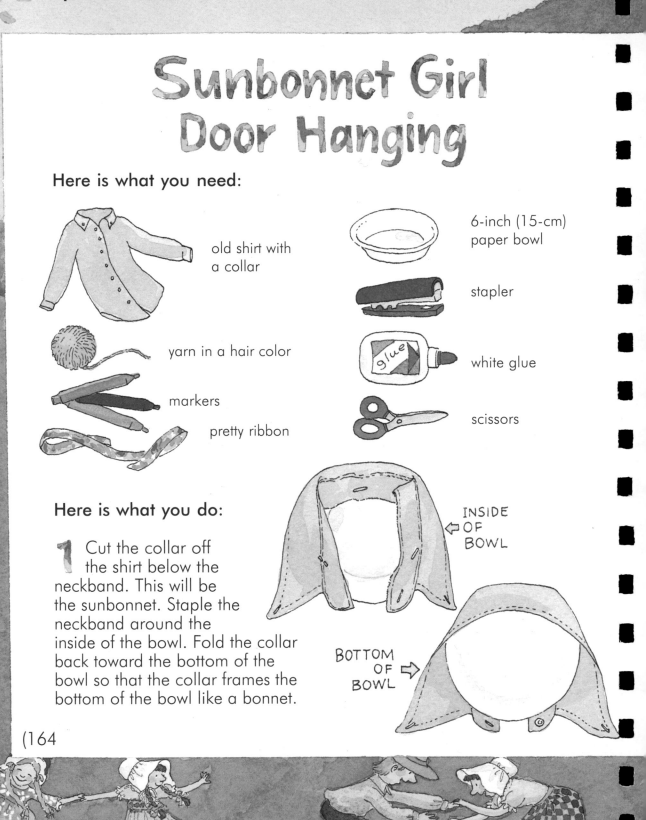

old shirt with a collar

yarn in a hair color

markers

pretty ribbon

6-inch (15-cm) paper bowl

stapler

white glue

scissors

Here is what you do:

1 Cut the collar off the shirt below the neckband. This will be the sunbonnet. Staple the neckband around the inside of the bowl. Fold the collar back toward the bottom of the bowl so that the collar frames the bottom of the bowl like a bonnet.

INSIDE OF BOWL

BOTTOM OF BOWL

(164

2 Use the markers to draw a face on the bottom of the bowl.

3 Cut bits of yarn and glue them around the face for hair.

4 Make a pretty ribbon bow. Staple the bow at the bottom of the face to look like the tied strings of the bonnet.

5 Cut a 12-inch (30-cm) long piece of ribbon. Staple the two ends of the ribbon to the back top of the face to form a hanger.

Hang this pretty little sunbonnet girl up for everyone to admire.

Summertime means lots of delicious berries to eat, but this project is a berry you can wear.

Strawberry Necklace

Here is what you need:

walnut

red nail polish

green felt scrap

plastic lid for drying

green yarn

scissors

white glue

Here is what you do:

1 Paint the walnut with red nail polish to make it look like a strawberry. Let it dry on the plastic lid. You may want to paint one side at a time to make sure you get a nice even finish all over.

2 Cut a pointy top leaf for the strawberry from the green felt.

3 Cut a 2-foot (61-cm) long piece of yarn for the necklace. Cut a slit in the center of the strawberry leaf. Slip the two ends of the yarn through the slit.

4 Glue the leaf with yarn to the flatter end of the walnut, with the yarn ends between the felt leaf and the walnut.

You could make several walnut strawberries without a yarn hanger. They are lots of fun to use for play food and look very pretty displayed in a plastic berry basket.

167)

This project can only be done on a hot day.

Melted Crayon Jars

Here is what you need:

 jar

aluminum foil

 old crayons in bright colors

ribbon

 scissors

Here is what you do:

1 Choose two or three different crayons in colors that look well together. Break the crayons into small pieces. If you use a large jar, you will need more crayons than if your jar is small. (Three crayons will cover a baby food jar.)

2 Tear off a square of aluminum foil. Place the foil outside in hot, direct sunlight. Sprinkle the crayons on the foil.

Lemonad 15¢/cup

(168

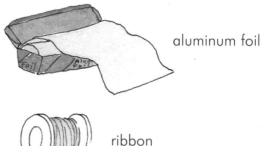

3 The crayons will melt quickly, so be ready with your jar. Do not wait until the crayons are completely melted or they will blend together to make a muddy color. When they have melted, but still have some lumps in them, roll the jar around in the melted crayons to coat it. When you are happy with the design on the jar, take it to a cool place. The crayon will harden and set almost immediately.

4 Tie a bow around the neck of the jar.

These jars are both pretty and useful containers for such things as flowers, pencils, and odds and ends. They are fun and easy to make and each one is different. Remember to keep your finished jars out of direct sunlight or the crayon coating will melt again.

169)

The earth is full of creepy, crawly things to watch on lazy summer days.

Friendly Earthworm Puppet

Here is what you need:

- plastic cup
- flexi-straw
- green construction paper
- masking tape
- brown tissue paper
- white glue
- two tiny wiggle eyes

- Styrofoam tray for drying
- plastic margarine tub for mixing
- water
- paintbrush
- pencil
- scissors

Here is what you do:

1 Mix one part glue with one part water in the plastic tub.

2 Cut a 2-inch (5-cm) wide strip of brown tissue paper about as long as your straw.

(170

3 Paint the tissue paper with the watery glue. Roll the gluey paper around the straw to cover it. Carefully slide the wet tissue up on the straw towards the bent end so that it crumples together to form the segments of the worm. Do this until half the straw is exposed. Pinch the tissue paper over the open end of the straw to make the head of the worm.

4 Glue two tiny wiggle eyes on the head. Let it dry on a Styrofoam tray.

5 Use the pencil to poke a hole in the bottom of the cup. Cover the sides of the cup with strips of masking tape to create a better gluing surface.

6 Trace your hand on the green paper. Cut out three or four green hand shapes. Glue the hands around the cup with the fingers sticking up over the rim of the cup to form grass. You may need to use masking tape to hold the hands in place while the glue dries.

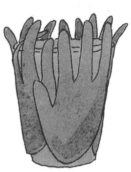

7 Push the uncovered end of the straw down into the hole in the bottom of the cup so that the worm is hidden down in the cup.

Push on the straw sticking out the bottom of the cup to make the worm pop up out of the grass and take a look around.

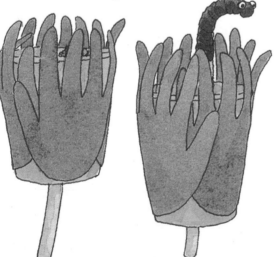

171)

Brown Bag Note Card

Here is what you need:

 two brown grocery bags (more if they're small)

 scissors

crinkle cut or pinking shears

envelope in the size you would like your envelopes to be

green and brown crayons

twine

 wildlife or other lick-and-stick seals

 pencil

small leaves

 white glue

Here is what you do:

1 Cut up the seam of a grocery bag and cut out the bottom of the bag so that you have a flat piece of brown paper. You will need to cut at least two grocery bags and maybe more. You can cut the bags all at once or cut them as you need them.

(172

2 Carefully unglue the seams of the envelope you have chosen and spread it out flat to use as a pattern. Trace around the envelope on the grocery bag paper. Cut out the envelope outline. Fold the envelope that you have cut from the bag at exactly the same places as your envelope pattern was folded. Glue the seams together, leaving the top open. Make at least four envelopes.

3 Make folding note cards to fit inside of each envelope by cutting them from the brown paper. To decorate each note card, put two or three leaves under the front of the card with the vein side of each leaf up, and use a crayon to make a rubbing of the leaves on the card. You can use more than one color to make the rubbing. You might want to experiment with the way you arrange the leaves and the colors you use. Do this on some scrap pieces from the cut bags. If you wish, give the note cards a crinkle edge using pinking shears or crinkle cut scissors.

4 To make the envelopes close, moisten only the top half of the seal and stick it at the point of the flap of the envelope. To close the envelope, the bottom half of the seal can be moistened and stuck to the envelope.

If you plan to give a set of cards away as a gift, stack the note cards and envelopes and tie them together with twine.

The dandelion is probably one of summer's most plentiful flowers.

Dandelion Corsage

Here is what you need:

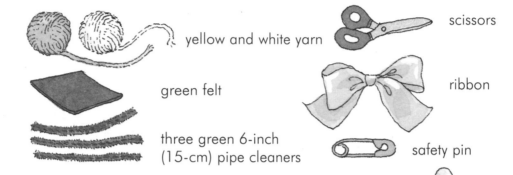

yellow and white yarn

green felt

three green 6-inch (15-cm) pipe cleaners

scissors

ribbon

safety pin

Here is what you do:

1 To make a dandelion, wrap yellow yarn around your hand ten times and cut the yarn.

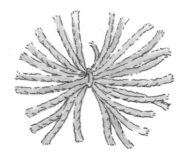

2 Slip the wound yarn off your hand. Tie it together in the center with another piece of yellow yarn. Trim the yarn on each side of the center to about 1 inch (2.5 cm) long.

3 Fray all of the yarn so that it looks like a fluffy dandelion. To do this, just unwind the fibers that make up each strand of yarn.

4 Hook a 6-inch (15-cm) long pipe cleaner through the yarn that holds the flower together at the center. Fold the end over the yarn to hold the pipe cleaner in place to form a stem for the flower.

5 Cut a 1½-inch (4-cm) circle of green felt. Cut little points around the outside of the circle. Cut a small slit in the center of the circle. Slide the circle up the stem of the dandelion to form the green cup of the flower.

6 Make three dandelions. If you want one of the dandelions to look like it has gone to seed, use white yarn instead of yellow yarn.

7 Cut two long, pointy dandelion leaves from the green felt. Cut a small slit in the bottom of each leaf. Slide the leaves up the stems of all three dandelions until they are sticking up behind the flowers.

8 Tie a pretty ribbon bow around the flowers. Pin a safety pin to the back of the ribbon so that the flowers can be worn as a corsage.

Surprise your mom with this pretty bouquet that will last for many summers to come.

175)

About the Author and Artist

Twenty-five years as a teacher and director of nursery school programs in Oneida, New York, have given Kathy Ross extensive experience in guiding children through craft projects. A collector of teddy bears and paper dolls, her craft projects have frequently appeared in *Highlights* magazine. She is the author of The Millbrook Press's Holiday Crafts for Kids series and the Crafts for Kids Who Are Wild About series. She is also the author of *Gifts to Make for Your Favorite Grown-ups, The Best Holiday Craft Book Ever, Crafts for Kids Who Are Wild About the Wild, The Best Birthday Parties Ever: A Kid's Do-It-Yourself Guide, Christmas Ornaments Kids Can Make, Christmas Decorations Kids Can Make, More Christmas Ornaments Kids Can Make, Make Yourself a Monster,* and *Crafts from Your Favorite Bible Stories.*

A resident of Andover, Massachusetts, Vicky Enright works at home with two large dogs and a small son. To date, she has utilized her talents as a calligrapher, a wallpaper designer, and a greeting-card illustrator. Her first book was *Crafts From Your Favorite Fairy Tales* by Kathy Ross, and she is at work on a follow-up, *Crafts From Your Favorite Children's Songs*.